The Gardener's Color Palette

PAINT YOUR GARDEN WITH 100 EXTRAORDINARY FLOWER CHOICES

TOM FISCHER   PHOTOGRAPHS BY **CLIVE NICHOLS**

TIMBER PRESS

TIMBER PRESS
Portland · London

Published in 2010 by Timber Press, Inc.

The Haseltine Building
133 S.W. Second Avenue, Suite 450
Portland, Oregon 97204-3527
www.timberpress.com

2 The Quadrant
135 Salusbury Road
London NW6 6RJ
www.timberpress.co.uk

Printed in China

ISBN-13: 978-1-60469-084-2

Catalog records for this book are available
from the Library of Congress
and the British Library.

KEY TO PLANT CARE SYMBOLS

LIGHT REQUIREMENTS

 SUN
Plant receives six hours or more
of direct sun every day.

 PART SUN
Plant receives three to six hours
of direct sun every day.

 LIGHT SHADE
Plant receives less than three hours
of direct sun and gets dappled sun
at other times during the day.

 SHADE
Plant receives little or no
direct sun, only dappled sun.

MOISTURE REQUIREMENTS

 HEAVY
Plant needs constantly moist soil.
Watering may be necessary during
dry spells.

 MODERATE
Plant needs moderate moisture.
Occasional watering may be
necessary during dry spells

 LIGHT
Plant tolerates some dryness.
Watering necessary only during
prolonged drought or heat waves.

CONTENTS

INTRODUCTION

Forget sunsets, precious stones, and butterflies. Flowers are nature's most direct and accessible route to enjoying the pure pleasures of color. In fact, it's impossible to even think about flowers without thinking about color as well. Say the word sunflower and your mind is flooded with yellow; talk about gentians and you conjure up blue at its most intense and dazzling.

I chose the flowers featured in this book because they embody color with a particular intensity or flair. Of course they're also good performers and mixers in the garden, and each entry mentions possible companion plants. But my hope is that you'll take the time to look closely at these flowers as individuals—as representatives of red, models of mauve, personifications of peach. After all, a flower is an object of contemplation as well as a denizen of the garden. You can be an urban apartment dweller without a square foot of soil to your name and still stand in rapture before the perfection of a single lily in a vase. And if you're a gardener, well, the opportunities for reveling in the flowers featured here are practically indecent (in the best possible way).

You'll notice that some flowers—tulips, coneflowers, and fritillaries, for example—appear in more than one color category. I make no apologies for this; some flowers simply have a talent, if I may put it that way, for playing multiple color roles.

Each entry gives you the essential information you need to grow the plant and describes those qualities that make the plant an especially apt embodiment of its particular color. You'll find each plant's botanical and common name (and how to pronounce the botanical name); what type of plant it is (bulb, shrub, perennial, etc.); the plant's height and spread; its bloom time; its hardiness zones (in other words, where it can be successfully grown); whether it's a North American native plant; and how much light and moisture it needs. If you fall in love with a particular plant and can't find it at your local nursery or garden center, your best bet is to track it down on the Internet—there are scores of mail-order nurseries that specialize in unusual and hard-to-find plants.

Words, of course, are a poor substitute for the actual experience of color—that intricate interplay of light, eye, and brain—so I suggest you turn the page and immerse yourself in the one hundred flowers that have been gathered for you in this miniature garden of earthly delights.

Red

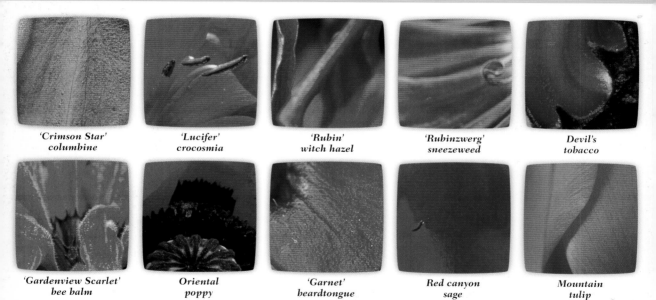

**'Crimson Star'
columbine**

**'Lucifer'
crocosmia**

**'Rubin'
witch hazel**

**'Rubinzwerg'
sneezeweed**

**Devil's
tobacco**

**'Gardenview Scarlet'
bee balm**

**Oriental
poppy**

**'Garnet'
beardtongue**

**Red canyon
sage**

**Mountain
tulip**

11

IT CAN BE A WARNING OR AN ALLUREMENT, a sign of passion or anger, of royalty or warfare. Whatever symbolic baggage it may carry, red is unequalled among colors for the sheer visceral excitement it provokes. For that very reason, some gardeners find it vulgar and strident. They don't know what they're missing. Or maybe they do, and simply don't feel a need in their well-regulated souls for the splendor of scarlet tulips, the unabashed exuberance of Oriental poppies, the jewel-like glow of crocosmias. But a garden without red flowers is a chilly place indeed. I say, let's turn up the heat.

Aquilegia 'Crimson Star'
'Crimson Star' columbine

PRONOUNCED **ak-wih-LEE-jee-uh**

TYPE OF PLANT **Hardy perennial**

HEIGHT AND SPREAD **18–30 in. × 18 in.**

BLOOM TIME **Late spring to early summer**

ZONE **3–9**

NORTH AMERICAN NATIVE

Sun

Part Sun

Light Shade

Moderate

IT'S STRANGE TO THINK OF THIS PLANT as a selection of the normally blue-and-white Rocky Mountain columbine, *Aquilegia coerulea*, but that, apparently, is what 'Crimson Star' is. Once the flower opens, the kinship is a bit more apparent, since the blades of the flower are white, contrasting beautifully with red sepals and spurs. Bright red doesn't usually give the impression of being a soft color, but it is so here, thanks, perhaps, to the matte silkiness that so many columbines possess. A late-spring bloomer, 'Crimson Star' is equally at home in a naturalistic woodland setting as in a border with other familiar flowers—peonies, false indigos (*Baptisia*), and bearded irises.

Crocosmia 'Lucifer'

'Lucifer' crocosmia

PRONOUNCED **kroh-KOZ-mee-uh**

TYPE OF PLANT **Hardy perennial**

HEIGHT AND SPREAD **24–48 in. × 12–24 in.**

BLOOM TIME **Midsummer**

ZONE **5–9**

Sun

Moderate

GARDENERS HAVE THE LATE British nurseryman Alan Bloom to thank for this eyeful of hot scarlet. As beguiling as the plant's fiery color is the graceful way its buds and flowers are held on the stem—in double ranks, with buds gradually increasing in size. 'Lucifer' is also one of the hardiest and earliest-blooming of the crocosmias, some of which seem to pine for the mild climate of their South African homeland. Not 'Lucifer', which will allow even zone 5 gardeners the opportunity to marvel at its combination of brashness and delicacy. For an airy effect, try it with a fine-textured ornamental grass, or for drama, with a dark blue-violet delphinium.

Hamamelis ×intermedia 'Rubin'
'Rubin' witch hazel

PRONOUNCED **ham-uh-MEE-lis in-ter-MEE-dee-uh**

TYPE OF PLANT **Hardy deciduous shrub**

HEIGHT AND SPREAD **8–12 ft. × 8–12 ft.**

BLOOM TIME **Late winter to early spring**

ZONE **5–8**

Sun

Part Sun

Light Shade

Moderate

WITCH HAZELS HAVE BEEN KNOWN to keep gardeners from committing acts of desperation as frigid January gives way to loathsome February. With their abundant, delicate, warm-colored (and often spicily fragrant) flowers, they provide cheer in the garden just when it's most needed. You can have your pick of sparkling yellows or mellow oranges, but the ruby reds ('Rubin' means ruby in German) are what really get your pulse racing, particularly if the bush can be sited where the low rays of the winter sun will catch the flowers. No cathedral boasts stained glass more beautiful. Witch hazels look most at home on the edge of a woodland, where they get enough sun to encourage heavy bloom.

Helenium 'Rubinzwerg'
'Rubinzwerg' sneezeweed

PRONOUNCED **hel-EE-nee-um**

TYPE OF PLANT **Hardy perennial**

HEIGHT AND SPREAD **24–36 in. × 24 in.**

BLOOM TIME **Mid-summer to early fall**

ZONE **3–9**

NORTH AMERICAN NATIVE

Sun

Heavy

Moderate

YOU HAVE TO WONDER whether the name "sneezeweed" has kept the heleniums from being more popular. (They do *not* provoke allergies, by the way.) That would be a shame, because their jaunty bearing and rich colors are perfectly suited to the gardening year's warmest months. Some of the taller sneezeweeds need staking, but not 'Rubinzwerg' (it means "ruby dwarf" in German), which is perfect for making a bright splash against a backdrop of ornamental grasses or taller prairie perennials. Most of the named sneezeweed varieties trace their ancestry back to *Helenium autumnale*, a tough daisy relative native to most of North America.

Lobelia tupa
Devil's tobacco

PRONOUNCED **low-BEE-lee-uh TOO-puh**

TYPE OF PLANT **Tender perennial**

HEIGHT AND SPREAD **5–6 ft. × 3 ft.**

BLOOM TIME **Late summer to mid-fall**

ZONE **8–10**

Sun

Part Sun

Moderate

IT TAKES A PRACTICED EYE to see the similarity between towering devil's tobacco and the dwarf, bright blue bedding lobelias, but kin they are. Native to Chile (and thus not exceptionally cold-hardy), devil's tobacco is both strikingly statuesque and, well, a little bit odd. But in a good way. It has an affinity for other Southern Hemisphere plants, like lily-of-the-Nile (*Agapanthus*) and red-hot pokers (*Kniphofia*), and its bold, elliptical leaves (which account for its common name) play well against finer textures. The arching, birdlike flowers, held in dark calyces, attract hummingbirds with amazing efficiency. Of course, they also attract us.

Monarda didyma 'Gardenview Scarlet'

'Gardenview Scarlet' bee balm

PRONOUNCED **mo-NAR-duh DID-ih-muh**

TYPE OF PLANT **Hardy perennial**

HEIGHT AND SPREAD **24–48 in. × 24–36 in.**

BLOOM TIME **Mid-summer to late summer**

ZONE **4–9**

NORTH AMERICAN NATIVE

Sun

Part Sun

Heavy

Moderate

POWDERY MILDEW IS THE SCOURGE of bee balms, but 'Gardenview Scarlet', selected by Ohio gardener *extraordinaire* Henry Ross, is reasonably mildew-resistant. It also does everything you want a bee balm to do: it provides a good eyeful of bright color in high summer, has a citrusy fragrance, and is highly pleasing to butterflies and hummingbirds. And if native North American plants are your thing, there's even more to like, since it occurs naturally from Quebec south to Georgia and from Maine to Missouri. Don't let it get too dry (that invites mildew) and if it spreads more than you want it to, just tear it up—it's shallow-rooted and easy to remove.

Papaver orientale

Oriental poppy

PRONOUNCED **puh-PAY-ver or-ee-un-TAY-lee**

TYPE OF PLANT **Hardy perennial**

HEIGHT AND SPREAD **24–48 in. × 18–36 in.**

BLOOM TIME **Late spring to early summer**

ZONE **3–9**

Sun

Moderate

Light

LIKE PEONIES AND TALL BEARDED IRISES, Oriental poppies are a sign that summer is almost here. Blooming at a time of year when floral beauty is at its most extravagant, they can hold their own against the gaudiest, most ruffled garden divas. For the truest reds, seek out 'Beauty of Livermere' or the Goliath Group, which look splendid near chartreuse euphorbias or a clump of dark blue or violet Siberian iris. Alas, this queen of late spring has a fault: the foliage goes into decline as soon as the plant finishes blooming. All you can really do is remove the dying leaves and grit your teeth until fresh foliage appears in the autumn.

Penstemon 'Garnet'
'Garnet' beardtongue

PRONOUNCED **pen-STEE-mun**

TYPE OF PLANT **Tender perennial**

HEIGHT AND SPREAD **18–24 in. × 18–24 in.**

BLOOM TIME **Early summer to early fall**

ZONE **7–10**

Sun

Moderate

THE BEARDTONGUES COMPRISE SOME of North America's loveliest wildflowers, but the named hybrids are definitely creatures of the garden, with a liking for softer living conditions than those endured by their cousins in the wild. But if they insist on good soil and regular water, they repay the investment handsomely, blooming almost nonstop for three to four months. Although there are plenty of whites, pinks, and purples to choose from, the reds—especially the deep ones, like 'Garnet'—have a unique sumptuousness that's heightened by purple foliage (try *Actaea simplex* 'Hillside Black Beauty') and deep blue-violet flowers (like those of *Clematis ×durandii*).

Salvia microphylla

Red canyon sage

PRONOUNCED **SAL-vee-uh my-kro-FILL-uh**

TYPE OF PLANT **Tender perennial**

HEIGHT AND SPREAD **24–48 in. × 24–48 in.**

BLOOM TIME **Mid-spring to mid-fall**

ZONE **7/8–10**

NORTH AMERICAN NATIVE

 Sun
 Part Sun
 Moderate
 Light

MEXICO AND THE SOUTHWESTERN United States are the home range of this variable sage, which packs a lot of chromatic wallop into its relatively dainty flowers. There are pink, orange, and even bicolor selections, so if red is what you want, it's safest to pick one that advertises the fact, like 'Forever Red' or 'Red Velvet'. Previously thought hardy only to zone 8, many selections are proving hardy in zone 7, so it might be worth sacrificing a plant or two in the name of scientific experimentation. Red canyon sage's relatively fine texture begs for bold-leaved companions, such as *Canna* 'Australia' (another scorching red) or *Eucomis* 'Sparkling Burgundy'.

Tulipa wilsoniana

Mountain tulip

PRONOUNCED **TEW-li-puh wil-soe-nee-AY-nuh**

TYPE OF PLANT **Hardy bulb**

HEIGHT AND SPREAD **4–6 in. × 3–4 in.**

BLOOM TIME **Mid-spring**

ZONE **4–8**

Sun

Moderate

Light

THERE'S NO SHORTAGE OF RED TULIPS, heaven knows, but the species (as opposed to the more familiar tall hybrids that populate most bulb catalogs) manage to combine gemlike color with a scale that makes them easier to use in certain situations, such as the front of the border, narrow beds, small containers, or the rock garden. Mountain tulip is one of many exquisite small species native to the Middle East (Iran and Turkmenistan, to be precise). When the shapely buds open, they reveal a small, shiny black spot at the base of each petal; a dozen bulbs planted next to a clump of gentian-blue *Lithodora diffusa* will make you dizzy with joy.

Orange to Peach

'Terracotta'
yarrow

'Orange Beauty'
canna

'Gwyneth'
dahlia

'Sunset'
coneflower

Crown
imperial

'Waldtraut'
sneezeweed

East Cape
poker

Henry's
lily

'Peach'
autumn sage

'Dordogne'
single late tulip

It WASN'T TOO LONG AGO that orange was considered anathema in many gardens. Thank goodness we've come to our senses, because orange is pure visual fun. It brings tropical warmth and brilliance into temperate gardens, and begs to be combined with other sharp colors: magenta, bright yellow, electric blue. Orange goes with margaritas and music that has a really good beat. As it modulates toward peach and melon, it becomes another creature entirely, losing none of its glow but acquiring more social graces, like a practiced hostess at a large party: "Miss Peach, allow me to introduce you to Mr. Brown and Miss Lilac. May I pour you some tea?"

Achillea 'Terracotta'
'Terracotta' yarrow

PRONOUNCED **ak-ih-LEE-uh**

TYPE OF PLANT **Hardy perennial**

HEIGHT AND SPREAD **24–36 in. × 30 in.**

BLOOM TIME **Mid-summer**

ZONE **3–8**

NORTH AMERICAN NATIVE

Sun

Part Sun

Moderate

NOT ALL YARROWS ARE CREATED EQUAL. Some are weedy, some fade, some flop, and some are just plain boring. But the good ones, like 'Terracotta', are very, very good. True, 'Terracotta' is most vivid right after the buds open, but the flowers lighten to a subtle and harmonious shade, almost a buff, that accords nicely with the deep orange newer flowers. Its earthy tones conjure up visions of sun-baked western landscapes, where wispy plants like Mexican feather grass (*Nassella tenuissima*) keep company with sculptural succulents like yuccas and agaves. Another possibility would be to create a hardy "Mediterranean" scene with lavenders and bear's-breeches (*Acanthus*).

Canna 'Orange Beauty'
'Orange Beauty' canna

PRONOUNCED **KAN-uh**

TYPE OF PLANT **Tender perennial**

HEIGHT AND SPREAD **4–6 ft. × 2–3 ft.**

BLOOM TIME **Summer to autumn**

ZONE **8–10**

Sun

Heavy **Moderate**

CANNAS—EITHER YOU LOVE 'EM or you hate 'em. If you're a hater, may I suggest you give them another chance, because they can be wonderful in the right setting. And what's the right setting? One suggestive of eastern splendor and tropical luxuriance, with maybe a tiny touch of decadence thrown in for good measure. The uncompromising hue of 'Orange Beauty' begs to be paired with chartreuse or black elephant ears, exotic-looking hardy gingers, or dinner-plate-size dahlias in the lurid color of your choice. But please, please don't plant them with traditional border perennials. The result would (or should) make you want to scratch your eyes out.

Dahlia 'Gwyneth'
'Gwyneth' dahlia

PRONOUNCED **DAHL-ya**

TYPE OF PLANT **Tender perennial**

HEIGHT AND SPREAD **4 ft. × 2–3 ft.**

BLOOM TIME **Mid-summer until frost**

ZONE **7–10**

Sun

Moderate

IF YOU'RE SKEPTICAL THAT ORANGE could ever be considered a "soft" color, you need look no further than 'Gwyneth'. A waterlily-type dahlia, 'Gwyneth' is a big girl, reaching four feet in height and sporting six-inch flowers. But though her proportions may be Junoesque, her personality is gentleness itself, and she'll consort happily with just about any other color you can name. My own preference would be to pair her salmon-orange with clear sky blue, the kind you see in some delphiniums and in blue sage (*Salvia azurea*). A carpet of blue plumbago (*Ceratostigma plumbaginoides*) at her feet would look ravishing at season's end.

Echinacea 'Sunset'
'Sunset' coneflower

PRONOUNCED **ek-ih-NAY-shee-uh**

TYPE OF PLANT **Hardy perennial**

HEIGHT AND SPREAD **12–36 in. × 12–36 in.**

BLOOM TIME **Summer through autumn**

ZONE **3–8**

NORTH AMERICAN NATIVE

Sun

Part Sun

Moderate

Light

IN CASE YOU'VE MISSED IT, we're in the midst of a coneflower renaissance (or maybe "coneflower efflorescence" would be more accurate). Hybridizers have been busily crossing purple coneflower (*Echinacea purpurea*) with its relatives (including *E. paradoxa* and *E. tennesseensis*, among others) in order to broaden the coneflower color palette, and the results so far have been impressive. The orange- and red-flowered selections, of which 'Sunset' is a typical example, are particularly yummy, and each new generation of hybrids has been showing improvements in color stability, flower form, and longevity. It's a treat to have a group of coneflowers for those situations in which pink simply won't do.

Fritillaria imperialis
Crown imperial

PRONOUNCED **frit-ih-LAIR-ee-uh im-peer-ee-AL-is**

TYPE OF PLANT **Hardy bulb**

HEIGHT AND SPREAD **36–48 in. × 12–18 in.**

BLOOM TIME **Mid-spring**

ZONE **5–8**

Sun

Part Sun

Moderate

CROWN IMPERIALS ARE NOT MODEST; they're imposing, stately, "look-at-me!" plants. This needs to be taken into account when you're deciding how to use them. Little, winsome things are liable to look silly in their august presence; better to pair them with large daffodils and tall early tulips. *Euphorbia polychroma*, with its searing chartreuse flowers, would be another good choice. Although tawny orange is the default color, you can also find yellows and near-reds. I think the oranges are just fine. Be sure to plant the bulbs in a spot that has excellent drainage, and don't go sticking your nose into the flowers—they have a mildly skunky odor.

Helenium 'Waldtraut'

'Waldtraut' sneezeweed

PRONOUNCED **hel-EE-nee-um**

TYPE OF PLANT **Hardy perennial**

HEIGHT AND SPREAD **48 in. × 24 in.**

BLOOM TIME **Late summer to early autumn**

ZONE **3–9**

NORTH AMERICAN NATIVE

Sun

Heavy

Moderate

WE HAVE GERMAN PLANT BREEDERS to thank for many of the most attractive sneezeweed selections. (Note: They *don't* make you sneeze! Really!) Some, like 'Waldtraut', display a charming two-tone pattern, as though someone had taken a paintbrush and lightly washed a deeper pigment over the base color of the petals. Although 'Waldtraut' shouldn't need staking, you can produce an even more compact, topple-resistant (and later-blooming) plant by cutting back the stems by one-third to one-half in late spring. Good companions include tall ornamental grasses and warm-toned yarrows and coneflowers, all of which help create the pleasant illusion that you're in the middle of a sun-drenched prairie.

Kniphofia rooperi
East Cape poker

PRONOUNCED **nip-HOE-fee-uh ROOP-ur-eye**

TYPE OF PLANT **Tender perennial**

HEIGHT AND SPREAD **36–48 in. × 24 in.**

BLOOM TIME **Early to late autumn**

ZONE **7–10**

Sun

Heavy

Moderate

EAST CAPE POKER STANDS OUT among its kin by virtue of its plump, oval flower heads, which give you plenty of orange to look at (along with a little bit of yellow). It blooms fairly late in the gardening year, and so finding suitable floral companions can be a challenge. Japanese maiden grass (*Miscanthus sinensis*) is one possibility, especially those selections with silvery flowers. The late great English gardener Christopher Lloyd liked to grow East Cape poker next to the bold, glaucous-leaved African honey bush (*Melianthus major*), which is an inspired pairing, both visually and geographically. I'd like to try it near dark blue anise sage (*Salvia guaranitica*).

Lilium henryi
Henry's lily

PRONOUNCED **LIL-ee-um HEN-ree-eye**

TYPE OF PLANT **Hardy bulb**

HEIGHT AND SPREAD **4–8 ft. × 2–3 ft.**

BLOOM TIME **Late summer**

ZONE **5–8**

Sun   Part Sun

Moderate

THE HENRY IN QUESTION is Augustine Henry, an Irish plant explorer who in the 1880s found this species growing in the gorges near Yichang in east-central China. For this he deserves our gratitude, because his lily is a real winner. It's tough, tall, and easily grown; a mature, well-nourished bulb can produce as many as thirty flowers. That's a lot of orange. The papillae—defined (not by me) as nipple-like structures—are a curious feature of the flowers, giving them a vague resemblance to starfish. Whether this inspires you to create an "Octopus's Garden" sort of fantasy, with mermaid sculptures and whatnot, is entirely your affair.

Salvia greggii 'Peach'
'Peach' autumn sage

PRONOUNCED **SAL-vee-uh GREG-ee-eye**

TYPE OF PLANT **Tender perennial**

HEIGHT AND SPREAD **24–30 in. × 24–30 in.**

BLOOM TIME **Early summer to late autumn**

ZONE **7–10**

Sun

Moderate

AUTUMN SAGE WANTS TO MAKE YOU HAPPY. It blooms heavily, and almost forever. And although we're concerned with 'Peach' here, it also comes in red, pink, violet, and white selections. OK, so it's not particularly hardy, but you can't have everything. The first thing to notice about 'Peach' is the particularly soft, glowing quality of the flower color. The second thing to notice is how well this color contrasts with the dark calyces and stems. If you duplicated this scheme in your living room, you'd get lots of compliments. In the garden, play up the contrast by pairing 'Peach' with dark-foliaged plants— purple coleus or (in a container) *Aeonium* 'Zwartkop'.

Tulipa 'Dordogne'
'Dordogne' single late tulip

PRONOUNCED **TEW-li-pa**

TYPE OF PLANT **Hardy bulb**

HEIGHT AND SPREAD **26 in. × 6 in.**

BLOOM TIME **Mid-spring**

ZONE **3–9**

Sun

Moderate

TULIPS ARE SPRING'S MOST VERSATILE color stars. They can do bright, they can do subtle, they can do solids, they can do patterns. About the only thing they can't do is blue, which is just as well, because a blue tulip would be gross. 'Dordogne' wins raves for its rich, warm blend of amber, coral, and gold, which from a distance reads as soft orange. If you want to play it safe, pair it with the clear yellow tulip 'Mrs. John T. Scheepers'. But if you want to take a walk on the wild side, try it with dark purple 'Greuze'. *That* will get the neighbors talking.

Yellow to Cream

'Coronation Gold'
yarrow

'Sandanzaki'
Amur adonis

King's
spear

Spike
winter hazel

'Walberton Yellow'
crocosmia

'Kondo'
fawn lily

'Lemon Queen'
perennial sunflower

'Corky'
daylily

Yellow Turk's-cap
lily

Golden
peony

CLEAR YELLOW IS THE VISIBLE DISTILLATION of sunlight, which is why it is always cheerful. A single daffodil is enough to dispel the gloom and depression of late February. Yellow is also versatile, pairing well with both saturated hues and pastels. It becomes intractable only when (as in so many summer-blooming members of the daisy family) it veers toward orange, in which case it needs to be gentled by paler yellows, greens, and perhaps white. Its most luscious manifestations, however, are its paler avatars: butter, cream, lemon. (Notice the culinary parallels.) These, the best of companions, are to be welcomed always and everywhere.

Achillea 'Coronation Gold'
'Coronation Gold' yarrow

PRONOUNCED **ak-ih-LEE-uh**

TYPE OF PLANT **Hardy perennial**

HEIGHT AND SPREAD **30–36 in. × 18–24 in.**

BLOOM TIME **Early summer to early autumn**

ZONE **3–8**

Sun

Moderate   Light

STRONG COLOR ALLIED WITH STRONG FORM is a winning combination. The bright, almost mustard yellow of 'Coronation Gold' may not lend itself to being paired with pinks and reds, but it gets along famously with other yellows, orange, buff, cream, and white, and looks stunning with deep blues and violets. And the plate-like shape of the flower head makes the perfect contrast to tall spikes, such as those of delphiniums. Another good pairing would be with tall spuria irises, which enjoy the same conditions (bright sun, lean soil) and whose colors are an excellent foil for the yarrow's. Not least among its virtues, 'Coronation Gold' boasts handsome, ferny, gray-green foliage.

Adonis amurensis 'Sandanzaki'
'Sandanzaki' Amur adonis

PRONOUNCED **uh-DOE-niss am-your-EN-sis**

TYPE OF PLANT **Hardy perennial**

HEIGHT AND SPREAD **8–12 in. × 8–12 in.**

BLOOM TIME **Late winter to early spring**

ZONE **4–7**

Sun

Moderate

A RARITY IN WESTERN GARDENS, early-blooming Amur adonis is treasured in Japan, where it's associated with the new year. Japanese breeders have also produced exquisite double forms, some (like the selection shown here) with feathery green ruffs surrounding the central ring of petals. These gems of the plant world (which can command staggering prices) are best treated like the treasures they are, and put in a sunny, protected spot where you can admire them at leisure and where they'll be out of the way of careless human and canine feet. If you manage to assemble a collection of selected forms, you'll be the envy of the gardening cognoscenti for miles around.

Asphodeline lutea
King's spear

PRONOUNCED **ass-fuh-del-EYE-nee LOO-tee-uh**

TYPE OF PLANT **Hardy perennial**

HEIGHT AND SPREAD **36–48 in. × 18–24 in.**

BLOOM TIME **Early summer**

ZONE **6–9**

Sun

Moderate

Light

WITH ITS TALL FLOWER STALKS and grassy, fountain-like foliage, king's spear is a prime candidate for a meadow-type planting that combines ornamental grasses with flowering perennials that have a wild (as opposed to highly cultivated) character. In that kind of setting, massive, overly hybridized flowers just don't work—they look gross and tawdry. The best choices are plants like king's spear, which provide small bursts of clear color against the prevailing greens and golds of the grasses. A native of the eastern Mediterranean, king's spear is reasonably drought-tolerant once established, and consorts comfortably with other Mediterranean plants such as euphorbias and rock roses (*Cistus*).

Corylopsis spicata

Spike winter hazel

PRONOUNCED **kor-ih-LOP-sis spy-KAY-tuh**

TYPE OF PLANT **Hardy deciduous shrub**

HEIGHT AND SPREAD **4–8 ft. × 6–10 ft.**

BLOOM TIME **Early to mid-spring**

ZONE **5–8**

Part Sun   Light Shade

Moderate

IN A PERFECT WORLD, GARDENERS WOULD DIG up their forsythias and plant winter hazels, which provide the same abundance of bloom in a delicate shade of yellow that accords much better with the sharp greens and bronzes of emerging foliage. That will never happen, but even a small increase in the number of winter hazels in the landscape would be a step in the right direction. Thanks to their gentle coloration, winter hazels combine well with just about any other color, but a particularly inspired pairing can be seen at Winterthur in Delaware, where Henry Francis du Pont interplanted his winter hazels with Korean rhododendron (*Rhododendron mucronulatum*), whose flowers are a strong rosy lavender. Magic.

Crocosmia 'Walberton Yellow'

'Walberton Yellow' crocosmia

PRONOUNCED **kroh-KOZ-mee-uh**

TYPE OF PLANT **Hardy perennial**

HEIGHT AND SPREAD **24–30 in. × 24 in.**

BLOOM TIME **Late summer to early fall**

ZONE **6–9**

Sun

Moderate

CROCOSMIAS ARE NEAR THE TOP OF MY LIST of "most underused perennials." True, some selections are a bit tender, but there are plenty that are hardy to zone 6 and some are hardy to zone 5. What's so special about them? The colors, of course—a wide range of warm, clear hues—and the fact that they bloom for many weeks in late summer. But their most appealing feature is the way the individual flowers cluster on the stems, which might remind you of their South African relatives, the freesias. 'Walberton Yellow', bred by British nurseryman David Tristram, exhibits the improved color, habit, and length of bloom typical of many more recent crocosmia hybrids.

Erythronium 'Kondo'
'Kondo' fawn lily

PRONOUNCED **air-ih-THROW-nee-um**

TYPE OF PLANT **Hardy bulb**

HEIGHT AND SPREAD **6–12 in. × 6 in.**

BLOOM TIME **Late spring**

ZONE **3–9**

NORTH AMERICAN NATIVE

Part Sun

Light Shade

Moderate

FAWN LILIES ARE ONE OF THE CHIEF GLORIES of spring on the West Coast of North America. If you're lucky enough to come across a field of them in bloom, you'll never forget the sight. 'Kondo' is the offspring of two exquisite species, *Erythronium tuolumnense*, from which it gets its yellow coloration, and *E. californicum*, from which it gets its brown central markings and beautifully marbled foliage. Use them with abandon, but remember that the foliage disappears soon after the plants finish blooming, so you'll need to compensate by tucking the bulbs between clumps of hostas, deciduous ferns, or late-blooming shade lovers like toad lilies (*Tricyrtis*).

Helianthus 'Lemon Queen'
'Lemon Queen' perennial sunflower

PRONOUNCED **hee-lee-AN-thus**

TYPE OF PLANT **Hardy perennial**

HEIGHT AND SPREAD **5–8 ft. × 4 ft.**

BLOOM TIME **Mid- to late summer**

ZONE **3–9**

NORTH AMERICAN NATIVE

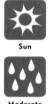

Sun

Moderate

IF YOU HAVE ROOM FOR ONLY ONE LARGE PERENNIAL in your garden, let it be 'Lemon Queen'. This peerless selection of a naturally occurring midwestern hybrid sunflower is about as reliable and care-free as a perennial gets. The first buds begin to open in mid-summer and then day by day the pace gains momentum until the plant becomes a fountain of clear yellow flowers. Although light yellow is about as versatile as a color can be, it reaches its peak of beauty when juxtaposed with other clear, light colors: cool pinks, lavenders, light blues, and white. Asters, phloxes, scabious (*Scabiosa*), and tall burnets (*Sanguisorba*) would all fit the bill.

Hemerocallis 'Corky'

'Corky' daylily

PRONOUNCED **hem-er-oh-KAL-iss**

TYPE OF PLANT **Hardy perennial**

HEIGHT AND SPREAD **36 in. × 24 in.**

BLOOM TIME **Mid- to late summer**

ZONE **3–9**

Sun · Light Shade

Moderate

THE WORLD OF DAYLILIES IS VAST, and if you're an enthusiast, chances are you don't get too excited about old-fashioned selections like 'Corky', which has been around since 1959. But if you can live without huge, ruffled flowers and trendy new colors, you'll find that 'Corky' is one of the most elegant daylilies you can grow. Its clear, lemon-yellow flowers—a mere two to three inches across—are marked with bronze on the backs of the petals and borne on long, slender, brownish-black stalks. They are, indeed, lily-like, and much more flattering to a wide range of summer-blooming companions than, say, the latest eight-inch, liver-colored tetraploid.

Lilium pyrenaicum
Yellow Turk's-cap lily

PRONOUNCED **LIL-ee-um py-ren-AY-ih-kum**

TYPE OF PLANT **Hardy bulb**

HEIGHT AND SPREAD **12–36 in. × 4–8 in.**

BLOOM TIME **Early summer**

ZONE **4–7**

Sun

Part Sun

Moderate

THE DESCRIPTION "Turk's-cap" applies to any lily with reflexed petals and downward-facing flowers. It's a charming form that you don't see very often among hybrid lilies, which is why the species that display it are worth growing. The flowers of yellow Turk's-cap lily appear atop tall, densely leafy stalks, drawing your attention to the individual flowers, whose clear yellow is accented by a sprinkling of small purple dots. A clever gardener will take advantage of this contrast by pairing the lily with dark purple columbines or campanulas, or with the dusky mourning widow (*Geranium phaeum*). A clump of bright yellow thermopsis or baptisia would also do nicely.

Paeonia mlokosewitschii
Golden peony

PRONOUNCED **pee-OH-nee-uh muh-lock-oh-zih-VITCH-ee-eye**

TYPE OF PLANT **Hardy perennial**

HEIGHT AND SPREAD **18–30 in. × 24 in.**

BLOOM TIME **Late spring**

ZONE **3–8**

Sun

Part Sun

Moderate

GOLDEN PEONY HAS THE DUBIOUS DISTINCTION of having the most unpronounceable botanical name of any plant in cultivation. If those Slavic syllables (the plant was named for a Polish botanist) prove too much for you, you can always opt for the British nickname, Molly-the-witch. The fragile, shimmering flowers of golden peony are truly breath-taking; the fact that they last only about a week simply means that you need to set aside the time to enjoy them. Fortunately, the plant's foliage is attractive as well, especially in its earliest stages: the emerging shoots are a stunning reddish-plum color that looks magnificent among small early bulbs like crocuses and glory-of-the-snow (*Chionodoxa*).

Green to Chartreuse

'Jade'
purple coneflower

Green-flowered
pineapple lily

Sikkim
spurge

Levantine
fritillary

'Harvington Double
Green' Lenten rose

'Percy's Pride'
red hot poker

Nepal
lily

'Lime Green'
flowering tobacco

'Spring Green'
viridiflora tulip

Green
false hellebore

GREEN, OF COURSE, IS THE UNIVERSAL HUE of gardening. But something mysterious happens when it makes the jump from foliage to flower. Maybe it's just the shock of the unexpected, but green flowers unfailingly grab our attention. We may find them odd, exquisite, or hideous, but we cannot ignore them. Often the green in a green flower is allied with other colors—brown or purple or maroon—which makes possible all sorts of interesting combinations. And the variations in the quality of the green itself, from bluish celadon through yellowish chartreuse, are themselves fascinating. Incidentally, it is a universally acknowledged truth that chartreuse pairs stunningly with every other color.

Echinacea purpurea 'Jade'
'Jade' purple coneflower

PRONOUNCED **ek-ih-NAY-shee-uh**

TYPE OF PLANT **Hardy perennial**

HEIGHT AND SPREAD **24 in. × 24 in.**

BLOOM TIME **Mid-summer to early autumn**

ZONE **3–9**

NORTH AMERICAN NATIVE

Sun

Part Sun

Moderate

WHICH CONEFLOWERS ARE THE MOST BEAUTIFUL? The familiar rosy pinks? The new sunset colors? Or the pale, ghostly whites, creams, and greens? It is, of course, a matter of personal taste, but 'Jade' has an ethereal beauty, like fine celadon porcelain, that puts it in a class of its own. Green flowers, in general, need careful placement if they're not to disappear among into the matrix of surrounding foliage, so give 'Jade' bright, contrasting companions, such as hot pink phloxes or astilbes, or, alternatively, plant large drifts among fine-textured grasses like hair grass (*Deschampsia cespitosa*) or Mexican feather grass (*Nassella tenuissima*), which will underscore the coneflower's distinctive shape.

Eucomis bicolor 'Alba'
Green-flowered pineapple lily

PRONOUNCED **YOO-kum-iss BY-kul-ur**

TYPE OF PLANT **Tender perennial**

HEIGHT AND SPREAD **18–24 in. × 24–30 in.**

BLOOM TIME **Mid-summer to early autumn**

ZONE **6/7–10**

Sun

Moderate

THERE ARE FASHIONS IN THE WORLD OF GARDENING, as there are everywhere else in modern life, and pineapple lilies are currently enjoying a surge in popularity. For one thing, they're turning out to be hardier than previously thought, and their striking architectural presence is in tune with contemporary sensibilities. But we're concerned mainly with color here, and green-flowered pineapple lily is as cool a customer as you'll find among the group. (The flowers of the ordinary species are edged with dark purple, which you may actually prefer.) My inclination would be to forgo companion plants and use it as a specimen to be admired for its color and form.

Euphorbia sikkimensis
Sikkim spurge

PRONOUNCED **yoo-FOR-bee-uh sick-im-EN-siss**

TYPE OF PLANT **Hardy perennial**

HEIGHT AND SPREAD **36–48 in. × 18 in.**

BLOOM TIME **Mid- to late summer**

ZONE **6–9**

THE HARDY PERENNIAL SPURGES can be divided by blooming period into early, middle, and late. The late bloomers, like Sikkim spurge, are the least common but also the most useful, since the flowers' vivid chartreuse makes a striking complement to just about any other color in the late-summer border. But wait, there's more! The plant's emerging shoots are bright pink (wouldn't they look good near some white or viridiflora tulips?), and when it finishes blooming, it's topped with attractive blue-green seed pods. That's quite a lot of ornamental value from a single plant. All spurges, when cut, bleed a sticky white latex that can irritate the skin and eyes, so wear gloves when handling them.

Fritillaria acmopetala
Levantine fritillary

PRONOUNCED **frit-ill-AIR-ee-uh ack-mo-PET-uh-luh**

TYPE OF PLANT **Hardy bulb**

HEIGHT AND SPREAD **12–24 in. × 6–8 in.**

BLOOM TIME **Mid- to late spring**

ZONE **6–10**

Sun

Part Sun

Light Shade

Moderate

SOME OF THE MOST BEAUTIFUL GREEN FLOWERS aren't entirely green; small touches of a contrasting color—like the purple-brown markings on the petals of Levantine fritillary—serve to underscore the singularity of the flower's coloration. Like many of its kin, Levantine fritillary specializes in the more subdued segments of the spectrum, and so should be planted where it can be admired at close range. (And don't place it near bright flowers that might steal the show.) Although some fritillaries are notoriously difficult to grow, this eastern Mediterranean species is one of the easiest, and will often self-sow, though never to the point of becoming a nuisance.

Helleborus ×hybridus 'Harvington Double Green'
'Harvington Double Green' Lenten rose

PRONOUNCED **heh-LEB-ur-us HIB-rih-dus**

TYPE OF PLANT **Hardy perennial**

HEIGHT AND SPREAD **12–18 in. × 18–30 in.**

BLOOM TIME **Early spring**

ZONE **4–9**

Light Shade Full Shade

Moderate

WE'RE LIVING IN A GOLDEN AGE OF HELLEBORES. Not that long ago, the only plants you could find for sale had muddy, miserable flowers. Now they can be had in a sumptuous array of rich colors and in a variety of forms: single, double, or even anemone-flowered. You might not be able to find 'Harvington Double Green' at your local nursery, but you will certainly be able to find a high-quality double green, even though it might not have a cultivar name. Green Lenten roses look splendid with their white and pink conspecifics, as well as with other harbingers of the spring: snowdrops (*Galanthus*), fumitories (*Corydalis*), and early daffodils (*Narcissus*).

Kniphofia 'Percy's Pride'
'Percy's Pride' red hot poker

PRONOUNCED **nip-HOE-fee-uh**

TYPE OF PLANT **Hardy perennial**

HEIGHT AND SPREAD **36–48 in. × 24 in.**

BLOOM TIME **Mid-summer to autumn**

ZONE **5–9**

Sun

Moderate

Light

WHAT DO YOU CALL A RED HOT POKER that isn't red hot? Anything you like, as long as it's evocative of cool loveliness. For all its elegance, 'Percy's Pride'—named for Percy Piper, a hybridizer at Bressingham Gardens in England—is not a demure plant, easily reaching four feet in good soil with adequate water. But thanks to its color, which hovers in a realm of infinite subtlety between pale green and pale yellow, it flatters every other color, whether hot or cool. My first choices for companions, however, would be dark blue lilies-of-the-Nile (*Agapanthus*) or monkshoods (*Aconitum*).

Lilium nepalense
Nepal lily

PRONOUNCED **LIL-ee-um nep-ahl-EN-see**

TYPE OF PLANT **Hardy bulb**

HEIGHT AND SPREAD **36–54 in. × 12 in.**

BLOOM TIME **Mid-summer**

ZONE **5–8**

Light Shade

Moderate

No, IT ISN'T THE EASIEST LILY TO GROW. But it's not impossible—the trick is to keep it as dry as possible in winter. If you have reliable snow cover, you're all set; if not, you'll need to dig up the bulbs and store them in a cool, dark place until spring. Is it worth the trouble? That depends on how badly you want to grow an impossibly exotic, headily fragrant denizen of the Himalayan foothills. My guess is that if you were to see a large patch of these lilies, catching the dappled sunlight coming through a light canopy of deciduous trees and shrubs, you'd think that storing the bulbs would be a small price to pay for such splendor.

Nicotiana 'Lime Green'
'Lime Green' flowering tobacco

PRONOUNCED **nih-ko-she-AY-nuh**

TYPE OF PLANT **Annual**

HEIGHT AND SPREAD **24–36 in. × 12–36 in.**

BLOOM TIME **Mid-summer until frost**

ZONE **All**

Sun

Part Sun

Moderate

SOME GARDENERS SHUDDER WITH DISTASTE when annuals are mentioned. They may be thinking of fat, blowzy marigolds, but not all annuals are garish, steroidal monsters. The flowering tobaccos, in particular, are epitomes of gracefulness. Some of the white-flowered selections and species are notable for their heady nocturnal fragrance (the better to attract pollinating moths), while others contribute color throughout the summer and into autumn, until frost puts an end to the display. Among the newer selections are intriguing shades of deep purple and brown, but 'Lime Green', which is hardly a newcomer, still wins top honors for versatility and likability. Use it to tone down hot pinks and oranges, or with whites, pale yellows, and other greens to create an ethereal summer tableau.

Tulipa 'Spring Green'
'Spring Green' viridiflora tulip

PRONOUNCED **TEW-li-puh**

TYPE OF PLANT **Hardy bulb**

HEIGHT AND SPREAD **18 in. × 3–4 in.**

BLOOM TIME **Mid-spring**

ZONE **3–8**

SCARLET AND ORANGE TULIPS ARE ALL WELL AND GOOD, but you may not want to have to put on sunglasses every time you venture out into the garden. That's when viridiflora tulips show their worth. These cool customers embody the freshness of the season. Like some of the fritillaries, they gain in effect by not being solid green; nevertheless, the broad green stripe down the center of each petal sets the overall tone. I'd be inclined to stick with subtle companions for 'Spring Green'—perhaps an ice-pink tulip like 'Pink Diamond'. At Great Dixter, his famous garden in southern England, Christopher Lloyd paired this tulip with the delicate umbellifer *Smyrnium perfoliatum*—a true stroke of genius.

Veratrum viride
Green false hellebore

PRONOUNCED **vur-AY-trum VEER-ih-dee**

TYPE OF PLANT **Hardy perennial**

HEIGHT AND SPREAD **2–7 ft. × 1–2 ft.**

BLOOM TIME **Late-spring to mid-summer**

ZONE **3–8**

NORTH AMERICAN NATIVE

Sun

Light Shade

Heavy

THERE ARE TWO THINGS YOU OUGHT TO KNOW about false hellebores. The first is that their pleated leaves are every bit as ornamental as the flowers. The second is that they are highly poisonous, and so perhaps not the best choice for the children's play area. Toxicity notwithstanding, green false hellebore stands out for the particularly luminous quality of its greenness. If the plant has a drawback, it is that it grows at a pace that could charitably be described as glacial, and hence is not often encountered at nurseries. If you see it offered for sale, snap it up, for it will bring elegance to any garden setting, formal or naturalistic.

Blue

Grecian windflower

'Père David' blue corydalis

Tall delphinium

'Picos Blue' sea holly

Chinese autumn gentian

'Gordon' netted iris

'Glacier Blue' Himalayan blue poppy

Grape hyacinth

'Blue Ensign' lungwort

'Guanajuato' gentian sage

LET'S BEGIN BY ADMITTING that anything blue is gorgeous: unclouded skies and distant mountains; kingfishers and indigo buntings; hairstreak and morpho butterflies. The list is endless, and near the top are true blue flowers, which ignite a gardener's passions more quickly than flowers of any other color. The great German nurseryman Karl Foerster, for whom blue flowers were almost a religion, made an interesting and important observation: "Blue," he wrote, "needs light." He was right—blue may look perfectly fine on an overcast day, but when bathed in sun it ascends to glory. And don't listen to the nonsense about not mixing true blues with purplish blues—blue, whatever its inclinations, goes everywhere.

Anemone blanda

Grecian windflower

PRONOUNCED **ah-NEM-oh-nee BLAN-dah**

TYPE OF PLANT: **Hardy bulb**

HEIGHT AND SPREAD **3–4 in. × 4 in.**

BLOOM TIME **Mid-spring**

ZONE **4–8**

Sun

Light Shade

Moderate

GRECIAN WINDFLOWER BELONGS TO A GROUP known as the "little bulbs" (as opposed to the tall hybrid tulips and narcissi). But just because they're small in stature doesn't mean that their visual impact is slight—a carpet of blue Grecian windflowers is a dazzling a sight as Wordsworth's "host of golden daffodils." The trick is to use them lavishly—not dotted about here and there and not as singletons or pitiful groups of two or three. No, they need to be planted by the score or the hundred. If you plant small groups of red, yellow, or orange species tulips among this sea of blue, you'll have a scene of Oriental splendor as rich as any precious Bokhara rug.

Corydalis flexuosa 'Père David'
'Père David' blue corydalis

PRONOUNCED **kor-ID-uh-liss fleks-yoo-OH-suh**

TYPE OF PLANT: **Hardy perennial**

HEIGHT AND SPREAD **8–12 in. × 12 in.**

BLOOM TIME **Late spring**

ZONE **5–9**

Light Shade

Heavy

WHEN IT FIRST APPEARED IN NURSERIES, blue corydalis caused a sensation: here was a hardy herbaceous plant with flowers of electric blue verging on turquoise. The enthusiasm lessened somewhat when it turned out that the plant needed rich, woodsy soil, constant moisture, and frequent division in order to thrive. If you can meet those conditions, then 'Père David' will settle down happily. If not, you may want to try one of the newly introduced cormous species, such as *Corydalis ornata* or *C. turtschaninovii*. They're scarce and expensive, but tough as nails and just as gloriously blue as 'Père David'. They all look splendid near the emerging chartreuse foliage of lady fern (*Athyrium filix-femina*) or golden hostas.

Delphinium elatum
Tall delphinium

PRONOUNCED **del-FIN-ee-um el-AY-tum**

TYPE OF PLANT **Hardy perennial**

HEIGHT AND SPREAD **4–8 ft. × 1–1.5 ft.**

BLOOM TIME **Mid-summer and early autumn**

ZONE **3–8**

Sun

Moderate

IT'S HARD NOT TO GO ALL TO PIECES over delphiniums. Part of it is the sheer intensity of the color and part is the majestic stature of the flower spikes, which tower over the border like gods and goddesses. Be picky about your plants. The Pacific Giant strain, the most commonly available group in the United States, is pretty worthless. You'll have better luck with a robust seed strain from a specialist nursery like Dowdeswell's Delphiniums in New Zealand. All tall delphiniums need good soil and frequent feeding, and yes, they may need staking. But when you see them in their glory, near tall lilies or phlox or meadow rue (*Thalictrum*), you'll know they're worth every ounce of trouble.

Eryngium bourgatii 'Picos Blue'
'Picos Blue' sea holly

PRONOUNCED **er-RIN-jee-um boor-GAT-ee-eye**

TYPE OF PLANT **Hardy perennial**

HEIGHT AND SPREAD **12–24 in. × 12–24 in.**

BLOOM TIME **Mid-summer to late summer**

ZONE **5–8**

Sun

Light

THE BLUE OF SEA HOLLIES IS UNUSUAL in that it comes not from the flowers, which are tiny and barely noticeable, but from the plant's stems and thistle-like bracts. And while it can be intense, it almost always has a metallic quality, which seems appropriate to the plant's spiky form. It pays to select your sea hollies carefully, since some species can be disappointingly pale. Named forms like 'Picos Blue' are usually a safe bet, and the more sun they get, the more vivid the color will be. With their lean good looks, sea hollies can seem out of place in a traditional perennial border, but pair them with Mediterranean plants like lavenders (*Lavandula*) and euphorbias, and you have a winning ticket.

Gentiana sino-ornata

Chinese autumn gentian

PRONOUNCED **jen-shee-AY-nuh SY-no or-NAY-tuh**

TYPE OF PLANT **Hardy perennial**

HEIGHT AND SPREAD **3 in. × 8 in.**

BLOOM TIME **Late summer to early winter**

ZONE **3–8**

Light Shade

Heavy

ALTHOUGH THERE ARE YELLOW AND EVEN SCARLET GENTIANS, the group as a whole is synonymous with the brightest, purest, most dazzling blue that nature is capable of producing. The autumn-blooming Chinese gentians, of which *Gentiana sino-ornata* is a prime example, are a bit particular about growing conditions: humusy, acidic soil, ample moisture, and bright light but not direct sun. If you can't supply these, try one of the easier members of the genus, like willow gentian (*G. asclepiadea*) or crested gentian (*G. septemfida*). If you are one of those lucky souls who can grow these living Asian sapphires, grow sheets of them and don't even think of diluting their beauty with companion plants.

Iris 'Gordon'
'Gordon' netted iris

PRONOUNCED **EYE-riss**

TYPE OF PLANT **Hardy bulb**

HEIGHT AND SPREAD **4–6 in. × 4 in.**

BLOOM TIME **Spring**

ZONE **5–9**

Sun

Moderate

IF YOU YEARN FOR TRUE BLUE in earliest spring, look no further than netted iris and its hybrids. With 'Gordon', you get two kinds of blue for the price of one: the light hue of the standards (the upright petals) and the darker color of the falls (the outward-projecting petals), which gains depth and richness from the small, bright yellow and white markings on the center of the falls. When you're deciding where to plant this or any other reticulated iris, keep in mind that the foliage keeps on growing after the flowers have faded and should not be removed until it begins to turn yellow. A bit untidy, perhaps, but those sea-and-sky-colored flowers are worth it.

Meconopsis 'Glacier Blue'
'Glacier Blue' Himalayan blue poppy

PRONOUNCED **mee-kuh-NOP-sis**

TYPE OF PLANT **Hardy perennial**

HEIGHT AND SPREAD **24–36 in. × 18 in.**

BLOOM TIME **Late spring to early summer**

ZONE **4–9**

Part Sun

Light Shade

Heavy

MAYBE IT'S A BIT UNFAIR TO INCLUDE one of the Himalayan poppies here, since they can be grown only where they can be assured of ample moisture year round and where summer nights are cool. (They are, however, quite hardy to cold.) But there is nothing else on earth like them—it's as though nature decided to fashion a flower from the finest, sheerest turquoise silk. To see one in bloom is to acquire a longing that never goes away (unless you're one of those lucky gardeners who actually *can* grow them). There is a bit of good news, though: 'Glacier Blue' is probably the most vigorous and robust of all the blue poppies, and might succeed where other selections have failed.

Muscari armeniacum
Grape hyacinth

PRONOUNCED **mus-KAIR-ee uh-ar-men-ee-AY-kum**

TYPE OF PLANT: **Hardy bulb**

HEIGHT AND SPREAD **6–12 in × 6–12 in.**

BLOOM TIME **Mid-spring**

ZONE **4–9**

Part Sun

Moderate

GRAPE HYACINTHS HAVE TONS OF CHARM; unfortunately, some (like *Muscari neglectum*) also have weedy tendencies and tons of messy foliage. But not this one. Sure, it will spread over time, but not rampantly. If you're looking for true, pure blue with no hint of violet, your best bet is to go with one of the named selections. 'Cantab' is a clear mid-blue; 'Saffier' is somewhat darker (and sterile, so it stays in bloom longer than other forms); and 'Valerie Finnis' is a strange but captivating icy pale blue. A group of any of these sparkling beauties planted near mauve or light yellow primulas would be enough to bring you to your knees.

Pulmonaria 'Blue Ensign'
'Blue Ensign' lungwort

PRONOUNCED **pul-muh-NARE-ee-uh**

TYPE OF PLANT **Hardy perennial**

HEIGHT AND SPREAD **16 in. × 12 in.**

BLOOM TIME **Mid-spring**

ZONE **3–8**

Light Shade

Moderate

MEMBERS OF THE BORAGE FAMILY, to which the lungworts belong, have a decided talent for coming in wonderful shades of blue. It's hard to imagine a shady garden without at least a few, especially since you get not only beautiful flowers but handsome, silver-spotted foliage as well. For companions, hostas and ferns—the usual suspects—are good choices, but try them with barrenworts (*Epimedium*) as well: their color range is broad and makes possible countless attractive pairings. If you find that your lungwort's foliage becomes mildewed after blooming is done, simply cut it off—new leaves will emerge and remain unblemished for the rest of the season.

Salvia patens 'Guanajuato'
'Guanajuato' gentian sage

PRONOUNCED **SAL-vee-ah PAY-tens**

TYPE OF PLANT **Tender perennial**

HEIGHT AND SPREAD **5–6 ft. × 2 ft.**

BLOOM TIME **Late summer to mid-fall**

ZONE **8–11**

Sun

Moderate

ONLY IN THE NEW WORLD DO YOU FIND true-blue sages, and gentian sage—as its name suggests—is the bluest of all. Some forms of the species aren't terribly generous with their flowers, but 'Guanajuato' provides them lavishly, and they are, if anything, an even more brilliant blue than those of the run-of-the-mill species. A nice bonus is that the triangular leaves have a small, purple central marking—not the sort of thing to produce goosebumps, perhaps, but a pleasant complement to the flowers. Companion plants need to have an intensity that can match the piercing blue of 'Guanajuato'; since it's a native of Mexico, why not try pairing it with medium-height dahlias, whose wild ancestors were also Mexican?

Lavender, Lilac, and Mauve

**Persian
onion**

**'Mönch'
aster**

**Milky
bellflower**

**'Comtesse de Bouchaud'
clematis**

**'Grosso'
lavender**

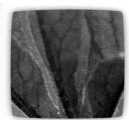

**'Willow Vale'
Spanish lavender**

**'Blue Spire'
Russian sage**

**Yunnan
meadow rue**

**Tall
verbena**

**'Apollo'
Culver's root**

WITH THESE SOOTHING COLORS, context is everything. In isolation, they sometimes lack excitement; it's creative juxtaposition that makes them come alive. Used with other pastels—primrose, peach, sky blue, soft pink—they evoke the freshness of spring, even at the end of a long, hot summer. But paired with bright, hot colors—scarlet, orange, strong yellow—they shed their demure personalities, like high school honor students who decide it's more fun hanging out with the tough crowd. The almost infinite variability of these colors has to do with the relative amounts of blue and red in their makeup, as well as the extent to which they are diluted with white.

Allium hollandicum

Persian onion

PRONOUNCED **AL-ee-um hol-LAND-ih-kum**

TYPE OF PLANT **Hardy bulb**

HEIGHT AND SPREAD **36 in. × 12 in.**

BLOOM TIME **Early summer**

ZONE **4–9**

Sun

Moderate

Light

THERE'S SOMETHING DELIGHTFULLY CHILDLIKE and innocent about the big-flowered ornamental onions, as if they had been drawn by small hands clutching crayons. The perfect roundness of their flowers is one of the plant world's most emphatic shapes, and one of the garden's most valuable assets. The mild lilac of Persian onion is an easy-going color; pairing it with pure white and deep violet (columbines or the shorter bearded irises would work) gives it a bit more oomph. If you go in for refined effects, plant it near an early-blooming perennial like cushion spurge (*Euphorbia polychroma*), whose chartreuse echoes the green centers of the onion's florets.

Aster ×frikartii 'Mönch'
'Mönch' aster

PRONOUNCED **ASS-ter frih-KAR-tee-eye**

TYPE OF PLANT **Hardy perennial**

HEIGHT AND SPREAD **24–36 in. × 12–18 in.**

BLOOM TIME **Early summer to autumn**

ZONE **5–9**

Sun

Part Sun

Moderate

BEAUTY AND ENDURANCE BOTH RANK HIGH among the plantly virtues, and it is a rare individual that has them both. 'Mönch' is one of those paragons, treasured as much for its clear lilac flowers as for its ability to bloom from early summer until autumn. The list of possible companions is, as you might guess, vast. In early summer, try Asiatic lilies and meadow rues (*Thalictrum*); in mid-season, lemon-colored daylilies (*Hemerocallis*), bee balm (*Monarda*), and dark violet campanulas; in late summer, phloxes and red-hot pokers (*Kniphofia*). Long-blooming shrub roses present yet another world of possibilities. To keep 'Mönch' in good fettle, give it rich soil and regular water—starvation and drought will most assuredly curtail its floral display.

Campanula lactiflora
Milky bellflower

PRONOUNCED **kam-PAN-yoo-luh lak-tih-FLOR-uh**

TYPE OF PLANT **Hardy perennial**

HEIGHT AND SPREAD **36–48 in. × 24 in.**

BLOOM TIME **Mid-summer**

ZONE **5–9**

Sun

Light Shade

Moderate

THE BELLFLOWERS ARE A LARGE AND DIVERSE GROUP, ranging from rock-garden tinies to boisterous border biggies. Milky bellflower belongs to the latter camp, and is famously generous with its floral display, which can range from pure white to pinkish mauve to fairly deep lavender-blue. The pick of the bunch is 'Pritchard's Variety', the darkest of them all, which has the added attraction of a white eye in the center of each bell. Milky bell-flower looks best in a traditional border setting with other soft-colored, old-fashioned flowers: yellow daylilies (*Hemerocallis*), pink and white astilbes, cranesbills (*Geranium*), trumpet lilies, and early border phloxes. If you let it, it will self-sow modestly, and may come up in unexpected places where it is surprisingly apt.

Clematis 'Comtesse de Bouchaud'
'Comtesse de Bouchaud' clematis

PRONOUNCED **KLEM-uh-tiss**

TYPE OF PLANT **Hardy climber**

HEIGHT AND SPREAD **8–10 ft. × 3 ft.**

BLOOM TIME **Mid- to late summer**

ZONE **4–9**

Sun

Part Sun

Moderate

THE COUNTESS, TO TRANSLATE HER TITLE, is a generous lady indeed, bestowing her large, textured flowers with aristocratic largesse. If you ever wondered what color mauve really is, now you know: it is light lavender with a good deal of pink in it. (It comes from the Latin word for the mallow plant, *malva*.) For all her floral exuberance, the Countess doesn't get excessively tall, and is easily trained on a trellis or tuteur. Ideally, this would be placed amid a group of tall, sky blue delphiniums and bordered with a short-growing China rose like 'Irène Watts' or 'Mateo's Silk Butterflies'. Sometimes soft and pretty is just what you want.

Lavandula ×intermedia 'Grosso'
'Grosso' lavender

PRONOUNCED **luh-VAN-dew-luh in-ter-MEE-dee-uh**

TYPE OF PLANT **Hardy subshrub**

HEIGHT AND SPREAD **30–36 in. × 24–36 in.**

BLOOM TIME **Early to late summer**

ZONE **5–8**

Sun

Moderate

Light

MOST LAVENDERS ARE, well, lavender, but 'Grosso' is almost a deep violet. A selection of a hybrid also known as French lavender or lavandin, it forms a large, vigorous, admirably tight plant. (The name 'Grosso', which means simply "large," refers to the fat buds.) 'Grosso' is no slouch when it comes to scent, either; in fact, its essential oil is used in the perfume industry. Want more? The flowers retain their color and fragrance superbly when dried. The key to keeping lavenders healthy is not to coddle them with humus and fertilizer and to make sure their soil is perfectly drained; spoil them, and they'll quickly depart for lavender heaven.

Lavandula stoechas 'Willow Vale'
'Willow Vale' Spanish lavender

PRONOUNCED **luh-VAN-dew-luh stow-EE-kus**

TYPE OF PLANT **Tender subshrub**

HEIGHT AND SPREAD **18–24 in. × 18–24 in.**

BLOOM TIME **Late spring to early summer**

ZONE **8–10**

Sun

Moderate

Light

A TRUE MEDITERRANEAN PLANT, Spanish lavender needs mild winter temperatures to thrive. With its conspicuous "dog's ear" bracts and sharp, almost medicinal fragrance, it's unmistakably different from English and French lavender. Many selections of Spanish lavender have flowers that are distinctly pinker than other lavenders, and some even approach magenta and crimson. This rosy glow, along with the plants' gray foliage, makes them ideal partners for pink rock roses (*Cistus*) and beardtongues (*Penstemon*). Mound-forming Mediterranean shrubs always look better when contrasted with sharply vertical plants—if you have room for some Italian cypresses or columnar boxwoods, they'll help make your garden look like a corner of Andalusia (or Provence or Tuscany—take your pick).

Perovskia atriplicifolia 'Blue Spire'
'Blue Spire' Russian sage

PRONOUNCED **per-OFF-skee-uh at-rih-pliss-ih-FOE-lee-uh**

TYPE OF PLANT **Hardy perennial**

HEIGHT AND SPREAD **24–36 in. × 24–36 in.**

BLOOM TIME **Late summer**

ZONE **5–9**

Sun

Light

WHAT ON EARTH DID WE DO BEFORE Russian sage came along? It's graceful, it's colorful and long-blooming, it has good foliage, it's drought-tolerant, and it flatters just about any other plant it's paired with. One of its nicest features is that the flower spikes remain attractive long after the small, bright blue-violet florets have dropped—they simply turn from bright lavender to pale lavender. OK, it does have one small fault: if you plant it in overly rich soil and water it too much, it will flop. So don't do those things. Although it partners beautifully with traditional border plants, it has a slightly wild quality that lends itself to grassy meadow and steppe plantings.

Thalictrum delavayi
Yunnan meadow rue

PRONOUNCED **thuh-LIK-trum duh-lah-VAY-eye**

TYPE OF PLANT **Hardy perennial**

HEIGHT AND SPREAD **36–60 in. × 18–24 in.**

BLOOM TIME **Late spring**

ZONE **4–7**

Sun   Part Sun   Light Shade

Heavy   Moderate

SOME MEADOW RUES ARE LIKE LIVING GAUZE—although they make a strong color impression, the flower heads are so open and delicate that you look through them as much as at them. Yunnan meadow rue offers not only airy, lavender flowers (exquisitely multiplied in the selection 'Hewitt's Double'), but dangling, cream-colored stamens as well. Such refinement demands companion plants that won't try to steal the limelight. In fact, you might want to stick with foliage plants like gold or gold-variegated hostas, variegated hakone grass (*Hakonechloa macra* 'Aureola'), or *Astilboides tabularis*. If you insist on a floral pairing, how about white martagon lilies (*Lilium martagon* var. *album*)?

Verbena bonariensis
Tall verbena

PRONOUNCED **ver-BEE-nuh bo-nar-ee-EN-sis**

TYPE OF PLANT **Tender perennial**

HEIGHT AND SPREAD **36–60 in. × 18–36 in.**

BLOOM TIME **Early summer through late autumn**

ZONE **7–11**

Sun

Part Sun

Moderate

WHEN TALL VERBENA FIRST BEGAN TO APPEAR in gardens, in the 1980s and 90s, it caused a sensation: here was a tall, graceful plant that could be dotted throughout the border to create a haze of lavender flowers that would last for months. (Another appealing feature: butterflies love it.) It's especially suited to informal plantings that emphasize texture as much as color: the wispiness of ornamental grasses, the round plates of coneflowers and other daisy relatives, the spikes of mulleins (*Verbascum*) and Culver's root (*Veronicastrum*). If you live in an area that's colder than zone 7, don't despair—tall verbena is easily raised from seed and can be treated as an annual.

Veronicastrum virginicum 'Apollo'
'Apollo' Culver's root

PRONOUNCED **vur-on-ih-KAS-trum vur-JIN-ih-kum**

TYPE OF PLANT **Hardy perennial**

HEIGHT AND SPREAD **4–7 ft. × 2–4 ft.**

BLOOM TIME **Mid to late summer**

ZONE **3–9**

NORTH AMERICAN NATIVE

Sun

Moderate

THE TERM "ARCHITECTURAL PLANT" can be vague and confusing, but it seems appropriate for Culver's root: the stalks are rigidly upright, and the leaves are held in tight, symmetrical whorls. The flower spikes themselves are long and narrow, emphasizing the plant's verticality. But even though the plant has a somewhat formal appearance, it's completely at ease in the company of free spirits like joe-pye weed (*Eupatorium*) and tall ornamental grasses (*Miscanthus* and *Calamagrostis* especially). 'Apollo' is a clear lavender that's utterly versatile; if a pure white is more to your taste, try his lovely sister, 'Diane'. Without exaggerating, you could say that they're both divine.

Pink to Magenta

'Summerwine'
yarrow

'Margarete'
Japanese anemone

'Purpurlanze'
fall astilbe

'Roma'
masterwort

Pale purple
coneflower

'Riesenschirm'
joe-pye weed

'Leonard Messel'
magnolia

'Alpha'
meadow phlox

Flowering
currant

Japanese
burnet

It's not all cotton candy and strawberry ice cream. Although pink can seem too sugary in certain settings (and has perhaps not been aided by its link with Mary Kay Cosmetics and the movie *Legally Blonde*), when used intelligently it's capable of both great delicacy and great strength. Pale pink inevitably carries associations of youth, freshness, joy, and spring. As it deepens, however, it sheds the chaste veils of innocence for the low-cut, slinky evening gown of experience. Hot pink and magenta don't take sass from anyone, and they're ready to show you a good time.

Achillea 'Summerwine'
'Summerwine' yarrow

PRONOUNCED **ak-ih-LEE-uh**

TYPE OF PLANT **Hardy perennial**

HEIGHT AND SPREAD **18–30 in. × 24 in.**

BLOOM TIME **Mid- to late summer**

ZONE **3–8**

Sun

Moderate

Light

'SUMMERWINE' SOUNDS ALL THE NOTES of its part of the spectrum, opening a deep burgundy-cerise and fading gradually to rosy pink. This is either a bonus or an annoyance, depending on your point of view. Since the colors harmonize nicely, it seems to me there's no need to complain. The yarrows' flat-topped flower heads are as striking in their way as the color of the flowers, and are useful for contrasting with the tall spikes of delphiniums or hollyhocks (*Alcea*) and with the mounds of cranesbills (*Geranium*) or the lower-growing artemisias. Plants with deep purple foliage, like some of the bugbanes (*Actaea simplex* 'Hillside Black Beauty' is a winner), present yet more intriguing possibilities.

Anemone ×*hybrida* 'Margarete'
'Margarete' Japanese anemone

PRONOUNCED **uh-NEM-oh-nee HIB-rih-duh**

TYPE OF PLANT **Hardy perennial**

HEIGHT AND SPREAD **36–48 in. × 24 in.**

BLOOM TIME **Late summer to autumn**

ZONE **4–8**

Sun

Part Sun

Light Shade

Moderate

JAPANESE ANEMONES ARE THE QUEENS of the late garden. Earlier in the season they pay the rent, so to speak, by producing mounds of attractive, divided foliage. Then, as autumn approaches, slender flower stalks appear topped with pearl-like buds. When the flowers themselves open, revealing their boss of bright yellow stamens, it's like the grand finale to a symphony that has already been going on for several months. It's probably safer to pair pink-flowered Japanese anemones with cool-colored companions—asters, monkshoods (*Aconitum*), and the like—than with brassy yellow daisy relatives. But if you're feeling adventurous, try for color echoes with the anemone's yellow stamens; it just depends on how much of a risk-taker you are.

Astilbe chinensis var. *taquetii* 'Purpurlanze'
'Purpurlanze' fall astilbe

PRONOUNCED **uh-STIL-bee chy-NEN-siss var. tah-KET-ee-eye**

TYPE OF PLANT **Hardy perennial**

HEIGHT AND SPREAD **48 in. × 24 in.**

BLOOM TIME **Mid-summer to early autumn**

ZONE **5–8**

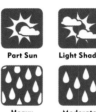

Part Sun   Light Shade

Heavy   Moderate

UNLIKE THE MORE FAMILIAR *Astilbe ×arendsii* hybrids, which bloom in early to mid-summer, fall astilbe waits a bit to put on its impressive floral show. But with this tough, elegant plant, the flowers aren't the only attraction: the deep green, fernlike foliage, held on mahogany-colored stems, looks good from the moment it appears in spring. Another bonus is that fall astilbe isn't as insistent on constant moisture as other astilbes. The most memorable combination using fall astilbe that I've ever seen was at Great Dixter, the garden of the late Christopher Lloyd. He teamed it with a light pink selection of border phlox (*Phlox paniculata*) and the towering stalks of a dark-purple-leaved annual amaranth. It was almost shockingly sensuous.

Astrantia 'Roma'
'Roma' masterwort

PRONOUNCED **uh-STRAN-shuh**

TYPE OF PLANT **Hardy perennial**

HEIGHT AND SPREAD **18– 36 in. × 24 in.**

BLOOM TIME **Late spring to early autumn**

ZONE **4–9**

Sun

Part Sun

Light Shade

Moderate

WITH THE MASTERWORTS, it's the collar of bracts that constitutes most of the "flower," and in the case of 'Roma', it's a clear light pink, inclining neither to mauve nor to coral. The true flowers, which might look like stamens to the casual observer, are a deeper pink, forming an exquisite contrast with the bracts. The delicate beauty of this masterwort doesn't lend itself to chromatically violent juxtapositions; try it with the blue-violet selections of *Salvia* ×*superba* or *S. nemorosa*, with Siberian or Japanese irises, or with silver-leaved plants like lavenders or lamb's ears (*Stachys byzantina*). Crimson coral bells (*Heuchera*) or one of the red-violet bee balms (*Monarda*) would also work nicely.

Echinacea pallida
Pale purple coneflower

PRONOUNCED **ek-in-AY-shee-a PAL-ih-duh**

TYPE OF PLANT **Hardy perennial**

HEIGHT AND SPREAD **24–36 in. × 12–18 in.**

BLOOM TIME **Mid-summer**

ZONE **3–10**

NORTH AMERICAN NATIVE

Sun

Moderate

Light

WITH SO MUCH ATTENTION being lavished on the new color forms of purple coneflower, the other members of the genus are in danger of being neglected. That would be a shame, because these charmingly simple wildflowers work well in situations where their flashier kin would stand out like a sore thumb. And although droopiness is not ordinarily considered a virtue in plants, the ray flowers of pale purple coneflower constitute a strong argument for letting your petals down. These narrow bands of pale lilac-pink would not be nearly as effective if it weren't for the large, maroon "cone," which also anchors and solidifies the flower. Don't try to make this wildling work with buxom border perennials; grow it in a meadow garden with grasses and prairie forbs.

Eupatorium purpureum subsp. *maculatum* 'Riesenschirm'

'Riesenschirm' joe-pye weed

PRONOUNCED **yoo-puh-TOR-ee-um pur-PUR-ee-um subsp. mak-you-LAY-tum**

TYPE OF PLANT **Hardy perennial**

HEIGHT AND SPREAD **5–6 ft. × 2–3 ft.**

BLOOM TIME **Mid- to late summer**

ZONE **4–8**

NORTH AMERICAN NATIVE

Sun

Heavy

Moderate

ALTHOUGH THERE ARE SOME "dwarf" joe-pye weeds, most of them are big bruisers and should be appreciated as such. When fully grown, they have as much visual heft as a small tree and can easily anchor a large, diverse border. In the color department, joe-pye weeds tend more toward the subtle than the searing. Their pinks and purples have a slightly dusty quality, which isn't necessarily a drawback; in fact, a hot fuchsia joe-pye weed would be terrifying— what on earth would you *do* with it? Far better to let their muted colors set off brighter companions like New England asters (*Aster novae-angliae*), bee balms (*Monarda*), and crimson mountain fleece (*Persicaria amplexicaulis*).

Magnolia ×loebneri 'Leonard Messel'
'Leonard Messel' magnolia

PRONOUNCED **mag-NO-lee-uh LOHB-nur-eye**

TYPE OF PLANT **Hardy deciduous tree**

HEIGHT AND SPREAD **20–30 ft. × 20–30 ft.**

BLOOM TIME **Early spring**

ZONE **4–8**

Sun

Part Sun

Moderate

PALEST PINK IS ONE OF THE COLORS that look best in the early-spring landscape, which is dominated by the sharp emerald green of emerging tree foliage and newly awakened lawns. Magnolias offer a wide range of pinks—some of them rather dingy, it has to be admitted—but that of 'Leonard Messel' is clear and fresh. And abundant: when the tree is at the peak of bloom, you can hardly see the branches. If you have the room to plant a small grove, you'll be dazzled by the multiplied gorgeousness of the massed flowers. To my mind, the best complement to 'Leonard Messel' is the simplest: clear blue glory-of-the-snow (*Chionodoxa luciliae*) spreading in a pool around the base of the trunk.

Phlox maculata 'Alpha'

'Alpha' meadow phlox

PRONOUNCED **FLOCKS mak-you-LAY-tuh**

TYPE OF PLANT **Hardy perennial**

HEIGHT AND SPREAD **24–48 in. × 18 in.**

BLOOM TIME **Mid-summer to early autumn**

ZONE **3–8**

NORTH AMERICAN NATIVE

Sun

Part Sun

Moderate

WITH THEIR SUMPTUOUS, ROUNDED HEADS of fragrant flowers, the taller phloxes are unfailingly seductive when you see them in bloom. Decidedly less seductive is the powdery mildew that can afflict some selections of border phlox. Happily, meadow phlox, which is every bit as eye-catching as border phlox, seems to be much more resistant to this scourge, even when growing in warm, humid parts of the country. The clear lilac-pink and emphatic shape of 'Alpha' make a fine, long-blooming foil for the spikes of the taller catmints (*Nepeta*) and veronicas, as well as for plants with cream-variegated foliage, such as the shrubby dogwood *Cornus alba* 'Elegantissima'.

Ribes sanguineum
Flowering currant

PRONOUNCED **RYE-beez san-GWIN-ee-um**

TYPE OF PLANT: **Hardy deciduous shrub**

HEIGHT AND SPREAD **6–12 ft × 6–12 ft.**

BLOOM TIME **Spring**

ZONE **5–8**

NORTH AMERICAN NATIVE

Part Sun   Light Shade

Moderate

A NATIVE OF THE COAST RANGES of California north to British Columbia, flowering currant has gained popularity far beyond the shores of North America. When you see it in bloom, you'll understand why: dense, arching clusters of flowers festoon the plant from top to bottom. They can range from pure white through the more typical pink to almost red. Flowering currant is ideally suited to a semi-wild setting, such as the edge of a woodland, and is flattered by the presence of other native western plants like false Solomon's seal (*Smilacina*). If you lack a woodland, it will be perfectly lovely with the emerging foliage of hostas and lady ferns (*Athyrium filix-femina*).

Sanguisorba obtusa
Japanese burnet

PRONOUNCED **san-gwih-SOR-buh ob-TOO-suh**

TYPE OF PLANT **Hardy perennial**

HEIGHT AND SPREAD **24–36 in. × 24 in.**

BLOOM TIME **Mid- to late summer**

ZONE **4–8**

Sun

Heavy

Moderate

JAPANESE BURNET LOOKS AS THOUGH it could have been drawn by Dr. Seuss—who else could have thought up a plant with flowers like pink caterpillars? (A friend of mine calls them "pink ticklers.") Fortunately, this element of whimsy doesn't detract from the plant's overall beauty (which is enhanced, by the way, by handsome, divided, gray-green foliage). Since all burnets like moist soil, it makes sense to give them companions with similar preferences. Dark blue monkshoods (*Aconitum*) would do the trick, as would the icy white form of mountain fleece (*Persicaria amplexicaulis* 'Alba'). Not many plants make you smile with pleasure; Japanese burnet is one of them.

Deep Purple, Maroon, and Plum

Purple-flowered onion

Korean angelica

'Sarastro' bellflower

'Petit Faucon' clematis

Mourning widow

Lenten rose

'Beaujolais' purple creeping Jenny

'Patty's Plum' Oriental poppy

Pasque flower

'Black Swan' single late tulip

DUSK, SHADOW, AND MYSTERY; silk, velvet, and damask. These somber colors invite comparison with night and luxurious fabrics. Observed at close quarters or held in the hand, deep purple flowers make superb objects of contemplation. In the garden, though, they're best used sparingly, to contribute depth and richness to lighter colors; en masse, they can easily slip from richness to stodginess. To use a different metaphor, think of the garden as a bowl of mashed potatoes and purple flowers as butter. You want the result to be sumptuous but not deadly. And of course you'd never dream of making mashed potatoes without any butter whatsoever—they'd be no better than wallpaper paste.

Allium atropurpureum
Purple-flowered onion

PRONOUNCED **AL-ee-um at-ro-pur-PUR-ee-um**

TYPE OF PLANT **Hardy bulb**

HEIGHT AND SPREAD **18–24 in. × 12 in.**

BLOOM TIME **Late spring to early summer**

ZONE **3–8**

Sun

Moderate

WHY THE SMALLER ORNAMENTAL ONIONS aren't more popular is a mystery to me. They may not be as shamelessly attention-grabbing as the huge, light purple onions such as 'Globemaster', but they come in a much wider range of colors: white, yellow, blue, and the mysterious dark mulberry hue of purple-flowered onion. They can also be easily tucked in among bulkier plants with a similar or later bloom period, allowing you to create intriguing late-spring compositions or to orchestrate an extended period of bloom in a single patch of ground. Given its somber coloration (thrillingly accented by black ovaries), purple-flowered onion cries out for paler companions such as white single late tulips or a single white peony like 'Early Windflower'.

Angelica gigas
Korean angelica

PRONOUNCED **an-JEL-ih-kuh JY-gas**

TYPE OF PLANT **Hardy biennial**

HEIGHT AND SPREAD **3–6 ft. × 2–3 ft.**

BLOOM TIME **Late summer to early fall**

ZONE **4–10**

Sun

Heavy

Moderate

NOT A PLANT FOR THE FAINT OF HEART, Korean angelica inspires awe for its imposing size, its deep maroon flowers and stems, and its uncanny ability to attract numerous species of alarming-looking wasps. (Remember what your mother told you: If you don't bother them, they won't bother you.) These dramatic attributes demand large, equally dramatic companion plants like Japanese maiden grass (*Miscanthus*, especially dark-flowered selections), Culver's root (*Veronicastum*), and joe-pye weed (*Eupatorium*). Because Korean angelica is a biennial or short-lived perennial, you'll need to think about how to fill the gap when the angelica goes to the big border in the sky. If your soil is sufficiently moist, you may get self-sown seedlings.

White to Ivory

'White Pearl'
bugbane

'Honorine Jobert'
Japanese anemone

White
crinum lily

'White Swan'
purple coneflower

Giant
snowdrop

Bowman's
root

Abyssinian
gladiolus

Christmas
rose

White
martagon lily

White
trillium

YES, WHITE IS PRISTINE and sparkling, but unless you're as talented a gardener as Vita Sackville-West, your all-white garden is going to be a big snooze. And, I might add, a cop-out—nothing is safer than to plant only white flowers. I'm not saying avoid white altogether, but use it as a painter would use dabs of zinc white: to brush in highlights; to balance or intensify other colors; to keep a complex color scheme from degenerating into chaos. And of course it's always revelatory to look at a white flower up close: did you ever dream that there could be so many variations of ivory, green, and pearl gray?

Actaea matsumurae 'White Pearl'
'White Pearl' bugbane

PRONOUNCED **ak-TEE-uh mat-soo-MUR-ee**

TYPE OF PLANT **Hardy perennial**

HEIGHT AND SPREAD **36–48 in. × 24–36 in.**

BLOOM TIME **Late summer to autumn**

ZONE **4–9**

Light Shade

Full Shade

Moderate

THE BUTTERCUP FAMILY, to which the bugbanes belong, has a knack for combining beautiful flowers with outstanding foliage. 'White Pearl' gets its name from the appearance of the flower buds, which open to small, fluffy flowers that form dense, icy white "bottlebrushes." Earlier in the season the lacy foliage might be mistaken for a particularly elegant fern. A selection of a Japanese species, 'White Pearl' joins the ranks of other choice late-blooming, shade-tolerant perennials native to that island: yellow hat flower (*Kirengeshoma palmata*), the toad lilies (*Tricyrtis*), false anemone (*Anemonopsis macrophylla*), and an exciting newcomer, trumpet spurflower (*Rabdosia longituba*). A gathering of all these plants would give you as exciting a shade garden as you could ever hope to have.

Anemone ×hybrida 'Honorine Jobert'
'Honorine Jobert' Japanese anemone

PRONOUNCED **ah-NEM-oh-nee HIB-rih-duh**

TYPE OF PLANT **Hardy perennial**

HEIGHT AND SPREAD **36–48 in. 18–24 in.**

BLOOM TIME **Late summer to autumn**

ZONE **5–8**

Sun

Part Sun

Light Shade

Moderate

YOU HAVE ONLY TWO CHOICES with Japanese anemones: pink or white; both are equally beautiful. But 'Honorine Jobert' is a nonpareil—the essence of all that is elegant, fresh, simple, and exquisitely formed. It's the floral equivalent of the Parthenon or the Taj Mahal. Even the buds are classically beautiful—like pearls balancing on long, slender stems. Although Japanese anemones don't kick into high gear until summer is slipping into autumn, they're an asset from spring onward, thanks to their attractive, dark green foliage. 'Honorine Jobert' will flatter almost any autumn-blooming plant, but you can create a scene of ethereal beauty by pairing it with dark blue monkshoods (*Aconitum*) and a blue-lilac aster such as 'Climax'.

Crinum ×powellii 'Album'
White crinum lily

PRONOUNCED **KRY-num POW-ul-ee-eye**

TYPE OF PLANT **Tender bulb**

HEIGHT AND SPREAD **24–36 in. × 36 in.**

BLOOM TIME **Mid-summer to early autumn**

ZONE **7–10**

Sun

Part Sun

Light Shade

Moderate

A WELL-LOVED MAINSTAY of southern gardens, white crinum lily is as indestructible as it is beautiful, producing its shapely flowers over several months and scenting the air with its exotic fragrance. It will thrive in almost any kind of soil, in sun or shade, and with abundant or little moisture. In fact, its only weakness is a dislike of being moved. Once planted, the bulbs should be left alone; the plants will increase in size and magnificence year after year, until they form a mass of deep green, arching foliage. Companions need to be able to stand up to the crinum's considerable bulk—large tropicals like elephant ears (*Colocasia*) and ginger lilies (*Hedychium*) will help perpetuate a sultry, southern mood.

Echinacea purpurea 'White Swan'

'White Swan' purple coneflower

PRONOUNCED **ek-ih-NAY-shee-a pur-PUR-ee-uh**

TYPE OF PLANT **Hardy perennial**

HEIGHT AND SPREAD **24–36 in. × 12–24 in.**

BLOOM TIME **Early to late summer**

ZONE **3–8**

NORTH AMERICAN NATIVE

Sun

Moderate

Light

WHITE FLOWERS REMIND US of the virtue of simplicity. Yes, it's now possible to find coneflowers in an array of exciting sunset colors and in fanciful crested and double forms. But 'White Swan' is so serene, so unaffected that it may well qualify as the most beautiful of the lot. Simplicity should also govern the way 'White Swan' is used. Try planting it in a drift in front of the golden haze of tufted hair grass (*Deschampsia cespitosa*), or contrast the flat plates of its flowers with the stark verticals of white Culver's root (*Veronicastrum virginicum* 'Diane') or the shaggy plumes of giant fleeceflower (*Persicaria polymorpha*). Above all, plant it in sufficient numbers so that its understated beauty doesn't get overwhelmed by flashier neighbors.

Galanthus elwesii
Giant snowdrop

PRONOUNCED **guh-LAN-thus el-WEEZ-ee-eye**

TYPE OF PLANT **Hardy bulb**

HEIGHT AND SPREAD **6–12 in. × 4–6 in.**

BLOOM TIME **Late winter to early spring**

ZONE **4–8**

Part Sun   Light Shade

Moderate

UNLESS YOU'RE A GALANTHOPHILE—that is, a snowdrop fanatic—it can be hard to tell one snowdrop from another. Giant snowdrop, however, stands out by virtue of its size and broad, glaucous leaves. If you turn the flower upside down and peer into it, you'll also notice that the inner segments have particularly bold green markings. The most spectacular display of snowdrops I've ever seen is at the Dunn Garden in Seattle, Washington, where enormous clumps of snowdrops are planted among ivy-leaved cyclamen (*Cyclamen hederifolium*), black mondo grass (*Ophiopogon planiscapus* 'Nigrescens'), and various selections of soft shield fern (*Polystichum setiferum*). It's a dazzling way to greet the spring.

Gillenia trifoliata
Bowman's root

PRONOUNCED **gil-EE-nee-uh try-foh-lee-AY-uh**

TYPE OF PLANT **Hardy perennial**

HEIGHT AND SPREAD **36–48 in. × 30 in.**

BLOOM TIME **Early to mid-summer**

ZONE **5–9**

NORTH AMERICAN NATIVE

Part Sun

Light Shade

Moderate

Light

SOME WHITE FLOWERS MAKE THEIR PRESENCE FELT not by sheer size but by delicacy and abundance. Bowman's root falls into this category. It may not make you gasp in amazement when you first see it, but it exerts a steady, subtle charm that ultimately proves irresistible. The flowers are a large part of the attraction, to be sure, but they're aided by the plant's dark maroon-colored stems, red calyxes, and the handsome seedheads and crimson foliage that follow later in the season. To top it off, the plant will grow in dry shade, that most challenging of garden conditions. For a simple but effective pairing, grow it with Indian pink (*Spigelia marilandica*), another charming North American wildflower.

Gladiolus murielae

Abyssinian gladiolus

PRONOUNCED **glad-ee-OH-lus MYOOR-ee-ul-ee**

TYPE OF PLANT **Tender bulb**

HEIGHT AND SPREAD **24–36 in. × 12–18 in.**

BLOOM TIME **Late summer**

ZONE **8–10**

Sun

Heavy

Moderate

IT WOULD BE HARD TO ENVISION a plant more distinct from the common garden glad than Abyssinian gladiolus. Whereas the flowers of common gladioli are large, heavy, ruffled, crowded, and often garishly colored, those of Abyssinian gladiolus are models of chaste design and presentation. And they have a wonderful, primrose-like fragrance to boot. Hardy only in fairly mild areas, they excel as container plants. Try grouping it with pots of both white and blue Australian fanflower (*Scaevola aemula*). If you want to grow it in the ground, just remember to dig up the corms before the first frost and store them in a cool place for the winter. Replant them in the spring after all danger of frost is past.

Helleborus niger
Christmas rose

PRONOUNCED **heh-LEB-ur-us NY-jur**

TYPE OF PLANT **Hardy perennial**

HEIGHT AND SPREAD **8–12 in. × 12–18 in.**

BLOOM TIME **Late winter to early spring**

ZONE **3–8**

Light Shade **Full Shade**

Moderate

ALTHOUGH CHRISTMAS ROSE ISN'T AS OFTEN SEEN in gardens as Lenten rose (*Helleborus ×hybridus*), its pure white flowers (which sometimes age to a warm pink) and compact stature make it an eminently desirable addition to the shade garden. Blooming as early as January in mild areas, Christmas rose can take a while to settle in and show its true potential, but the sight of a mature clump with as many as twenty flowers will surely convince you that the wait has been worth it. Not many other plants bloom as early as Christmas rose, so potential companions are few. Snowdrops (*Galanthus*) are a possibility, of course, as are foliage plants like black mondo grass (*Ophiopogon planiscapus* 'Nigrescens').

Lilium martagon var. *album*
White martagon lily

PRONOUNCED **LIL-ee-um MAR-tuh-gon**

TYPE OF PLANT **Hardy bulb**

HEIGHT AND SPREAD **36–48 in. × 10–15 in.**

BLOOM TIME **Early to mid-summer**

ZONE **4–8**

 Sun Part Sun Light Shade

 Moderate

IF, FOR SOME STRANGE REASON, you're not convinced that white martagon lily is worth growing, consider the fact that it has been in cultivation for more than 500 years. Better yet, just *look* at it. A single stalk can bear as many as fifty flowers, with their dainty, recurved petals and prominent yellow stamens. In the 1990s, I saw this lily being grown at the garden at Hadspen House in England. The renowned designer Penelope Hobhouse had planted a drift of them in front of a variegated pagoda dogwood (*Cornus alternifolia* 'Argentea'). It was a match made in heaven, and I promptly reproduced it in my own garden. Sometimes the best ideas are stolen.

Trillium grandiflorum
White trillium

PRONOUNCED **TRIL-ee-um gran-dih-FLOR-um**

TYPE OF PLANT **Hardy perennial**

HEIGHT AND SPREAD **8–20 in. × 12–18 in.**

BLOOM TIME **Mid- to late spring**

ZONE **4–9**

NORTH AMERICAN NATIVE

Part Sun

Light Shade

Moderate

WHITE TRILLIUM IS THE EPITOME of a spring wildflower. In the western part of its range, from the Appalachians to Minnesota, it can carpet the forest floor with white—a breathtaking sight if ever there was one. In cultivation it is vigorous and adaptable, as long as it is given rich, well-drained soil in part shade. Although much-coveted pink-flowered forms are known to occur, they don't surpass the white forms in beauty. Perhaps the best way to underscore white trillium's exquisite simplicity would be to combine it with two other eastern North American natives: blue phlox (*Phlox divaricata*) and crested iris (*Iris cristata*). It would be a way to have the glory of the eastern woodland in your own garden.

USDA HARDINESS ZONES

AVERAGE ANNUAL MINIMUM TEMPERATURE

Temperature (deg. C)	Zone	Temperature (deg. F)
Below −45.5	1	Below −50
−42.8 to −45.5	2a	−45 to −50
−40.0 to −42.7	2b	−40 to −45
−37.3 to −40.0	3a	−35 to −40
−34.5 to −37.2	3b	−30 to −35
−31.7 to −34.4	4a	−25 to −30
−28.9 to −31.6	4b	−20 to −25
−26.2 to −28.8	5a	−15 to −20
−23.4 to −26.1	5b	−10 to −15
−20.6 to −23.3	6a	−5 to −10
−17.8 to −20.5	6b	0 to −5
−15.0 to −17.7	7a	5 to 0
−12.3 to −15.0	7b	10 to 5
−9.5 to −12.2	8a	15 to 10
−6.7 to −9.4	8b	20 to 15
−3.9 to −6.6	9a	25 to 20
−1.2 to −3.8	9b	30 to 25
1.6 to −1.1	10a	35 to 30
4.4 to 1.7	10b	40 to 35
Above 4.4	11	Above 40

INDEX

Primula auricula 'Chaffinch'
'Chaffinch' show auricula

PRONOUNCED **PRIM-you-luh aw-RIK-you-luh**

TYPE OF PLANT **Hardy perennial**

HEIGHT AND SPREAD **6–9 in. × 8–10 in.**

BLOOM TIME **Early to mid-spring**

ZONE **3–9**

Part Sun

Light Shade

Moderate

THE SHOW AURICULAS ARE CREATURES of pure artifice—not that there's anything wrong with that. For centuries they've been bred to rigorous standards of perfection: the petals must open flat and display good color; the white circle of "paste" (actually, a mealy substance known horticulturally as farina) must be uniform and have a smooth outline; and the pistil must be "thrum" rather than "pin-eyed" (don't ask). Oh, and they're always grown in pots, because exposure to rain and wind would ruin the flowers. For all that, they're wonderful plants, worth coddling through the year in expectation of their few weeks of vernal splendor. 'Chaffinch', it need hardly be said, is a splendid brownish orange.

Rudbeckia hirta 'Autumn Colors'
'Autumn Colors' black-eyed Susan

PRONOUNCED **rud-BECK-ee-uh HUR-tuh**

TYPE OF PLANT **Annual**

HEIGHT AND SPREAD **24–30 in. × 12–24 in.**

BLOOM TIME **Early summer to autumn**

ZONE **All**

Sun

Moderate

'AUTUMN COLORS' IS NOT A SINGLE CULTIVAR, but rather a seed strain developed by the Ernst Benary seed company in Germany. The plants may bear red, gold, orange, maroon, or (as shown here) deep brown flowers. This variety is altogether delightful, and a welcome change from some of the over-planted perennial rudbeckias like 'Goldsturm'. Like many other annuals, the 'Autumn Colors' strain has the agreeable habit of blooming continually from early summer to autumn, provided the spent blooms are deadheaded. (Translation: Cut off the dead flowers.) If you want brown flowers—and they are a lovely, rich, warm brown—you'll need to buy the plants in bloom. Paired with orange red-hot pokers (*Kniphofia*), they'll give you goosebumps.

Trillium chloropetalum var. *giganteum*
Giant trillium

PRONOUNCED **TRIL-ee-um klo-ro-PET-uh-lum var. jy-gan-TEE-um**

TYPE OF PLANT **Hardy perennial**

HEIGHT AND SPREAD **12–30 in. × 20 in.**

BLOOM TIME **Late spring**

ZONE **6–9**

NORTH AMERICAN NATIVE

 Light Shade

 Full Shade

 Heavy

 Moderate

A NATIVE OF THE WEST COAST of North America, giant trillium is a true chameleon. The flowers can be white, greenish yellow, pink, deep red, or reddish brown. Some individuals are instantly forgettable while others are magnificent. The moral of all this is that it's a good idea to see the plant in bloom before buying it, since trilliums are slow to propagate and therefore expensive. The deep maroon or brownish forms benefit from being paired with bright flowers or foliage. The white-flowered form of mourning widow (*Geranium phaeum*) would be nice, as would Japanese painted fern (*Athyrium niponicum* 'Pictum'). If you want a more substantial partner, a not-too-huge rhododendron could work nicely.

Tulipa 'Abu Hassan'

'Abu Hassan' triumph tulip

PRONOUNCED **TEW-li-pa**

TYPE OF PLANT **Single late tulip**

HEIGHT AND SPREAD **12–18 in. × 4–6 in.**

BLOOM TIME **Late spring**

ZONE **3–8**

Sun

Moderate

IF YOU'RE OF THE OPINION that tulips should be red, pink, yellow, white, or some other "normal" color, chances are you're not going to cotton to brown tulips. If that's the case, you're missing out. The satiny sheen of tulip petals lends browns and coppery colors a subtle warmth and glow that those other colors can't begin to approach. If you decide to try them, however, you will need to adjust your tulip palette—pink and brown just won't do. But orange and brown, or deep ruby and brown, or darkest purple and brown—those are all thoroughly delectable. Another source of compatible hues can be found among the wallflowers (*Cheiranthus*). You can pretend it is autumn in spring.

Campanula 'Sarastro'
'Sarastro' bellflower

PRONOUNCED **kum-PAN-yoo-luh**

TYPE OF PLANT **Hardy perennial**

HEIGHT AND SPREAD **18–24 in. × 18–24 in.**

BLOOM TIME **Early to late summer**

ZONE **4–8**

Sun

Part Sun

Moderate

CAMPANULAS ARE LIKE THE LITTLE GIRL of the nursery rhyme: when they're good, they're very, very good, and when they're bad, they're horrid. 'Sarastro' (named for the Austrian nursery where it originated) is not only good, it's superlative. Its habit of growth is restrained, it doesn't need propping up, and it's covered for weeks with shiny, deep violet bells. This rich, sensuous color infuses life into companion plants with pink, lilac, or pale yellow flowers. Daylilies (*Hemerocallis*), lemon-colored yarrows (*Achillea*), and lavender fleabanes (*Erigeron*) would all be good choices. If you've had bad experiences with thuggish bellflowers like *Campanula punctata*, you'll be sure to greet 'Sarastro' as a welcome alternative.

Clematis 'Petit Faucon'
'Petit Faucon' clematis

PRONOUNCED **KLEM-uh-tiss**

TYPE OF PLANT **Hardy trailing perennial**

HEIGHT AND SPREAD **24–36 in. × 24 in.**

BLOOM TIME **Mid-summer to early autumn**

ZONE **3–9**

 Sun Part Sun

 Moderate

FOR MOST GARDENERS, the word clematis conjures up images of a fairly large twining climber festooning an arbor or trellis, but 'Petit Faucon' belies that stereotype: it's a compact, non-climbing herbaceous plant that can be allowed to mound up or lean against neighboring plants. Whatever its habit of growth, it's a gem. The dark violet buds open to deep violet-blue flowers with twisted petals, and the yellow anthers quickly mature to creamy white. Bloom period is a good three months, so 'Petit Faucon' can partner with a wide range of perennials and shrubs—pale yellow red hot pokers (*Kniphofia*), yellow foxglove (*Digitalis grandiflora*), and just about any of David Austin's shrub roses would all work well.

Geranium phaeum

Mourning widow

PRONOUNCED **jur-AY-nee-um FEE-um**

TYPE OF PLANT **Hardy perennial**

HEIGHT AND SPREAD **18–30 in. × 12–18 in.**

BLOOM TIME **Early to late summer**

ZONE **5–7**

Light Shade   Full Shade

Moderate

ALTHOUGH IT IS A DELICATE, retiring plant in most circumstances, mourning widow gains greatly in effectiveness when planted in groups of a half-dozen or more. The color of the flowers can range from pure white to lilac to almost pink to deep eggplant purple. (It's the darker colors that won the plant its funereal common name.) The small, downward-facing flowers are numerous enough to provide color echoes (or contrasts) with nearby plants—white or dark purple martagon lilies (*Lilium martagon*), common columbines (*Aquilegia vulgaris*), white selections of Siberian iris (*Iris sibirica*), and yellow lady's slipper (*Cypripedium calceolus*) would all make good partners and enjoy the same conditions (semi-shade, reasonably moist soil) as mourning widow.

Helleborus ×*hybridus*
Lenten rose

PRONOUNCED **heh-LEB-ur-us HIB-rih-dus**

TYPE OF PLANT **Hardy perennial**

HEIGHT AND SPREAD **18–24 in. × 18–24 in.**

BLOOM TIME **Late winter**

ZONE **4–9**

Light Shade

Moderate

ALTHOUGH MODERN LENTEN ROSES come in a wide range of velvety Victorian colors, the dark selections always seem to inspire the greatest enthusiasm. For some gardeners, the darker the flower—and you can now find almost pure blacks—the better; others want both dusky color and double petals. Until recently, this would have been a tall order, but deep purple, gray, and maroon doubles can now be obtained fairly easily, if for a price. If double Lenten roses remind you of miniature peonies, you're not hallucinating—they both belong to the buttercup family. When dark flowers are also shade lovers, it becomes essential to pair them with bright companions. White Lenten roses are an obvious choice, as are snowdrops (*Galanthus*).

Lysimachia atropurpurea 'Beaujolais'
'Beaujolais' purple creeping Jenny

PRONOUNCED **liss-ih-MAKE-ee-uh at-ro-pur-PUR-ee-uh**

TYPE OF PLANT **Hardy perennial**

HEIGHT AND SPREAD **24–36 in. × 12–24 in.**

BLOOM TIME **Mid-summer to early autumn**

ZONE **4–8**

 Sun   **Light Shade**

 Heavy   **Moderate**

As a rule of thumb, the creeping Jennys, or loosestrifes, should be approached with caution: most are vigorous, to put it politely, and some (like gooseneck loosestrife, *Lysimachia clethroides*) are pestiferous weeds. Purple creeping Jenny, however, is well behaved, so there's no need to forgo its fascinating purple-black flowers, which stay in bloom for almost three months. Another considerable asset is the plant's narrow, silvery foliage—a perfect foil to the flowers. Purple creeping Jenny lends itself to gorgeous compositions with blues, lilacs, whites, and silvers: think Siberian irises, false indigos (*Baptisia*), astilbes, cranesbills (*Geranium*), and Jacob's ladders (*Polemonium*). Is it a perfect plant? Alas, no—it tends to be short-lived, and will need to be replaced after a few years.

Papaver orientale 'Patty's Plum'

'Patty's Plum' Oriental poppy

PRONOUNCED **puh-PAY-ver or-ee-un-TAY-lee**

TYPE OF PLANT **Hardy perennial**

HEIGHT AND SPREAD **24–30 in. × 18–24 in.**

BLOOM TIME **Early summer**

ZONE **3–7**

Sun

Moderate

WE'RE SO USED TO SEEING BRIGHT RED and pink Oriental poppies that it can come as a shock to see one that's a deep plum-purple. And in fact 'Patty's Plum' caused a mild sensation when it first became available, with gardeners vying to see who could come up with the most creative combinations. At a nursery in southwestern England, I saw it grown near a purple-leaved barberry (*Berberis thunbergii* f. *atropurpurea*), and the chromatic match between the two plants was amazing. For floral companions, I can think of no better partners than purple and white foxgloves (*Digitalis purpurea*) and columbines (*Aquilegia*) in the same color range. Remember that Oriental poppies gradually disappear after they finish blooming.

Pulsatilla vulgaris
Pasque flower

PRONOUNCED **pul-sa-TIL-uh vul-GAIR-iss**

TYPE OF PLANT **Hardy perennial**

HEIGHT AND SPREAD **8–12 in. × 8–12 in.**

BLOOM TIME **Spring**

ZONE **4–8**

Sun

Light Shade

Moderate

JOHN GERARD, A SIXTEENTH-CENTURY English herbalist, praised this diminutive anemone relative for its "floures of great beautie," even though it had no medicinal or culinary "vertue." Modern gardeners will be inclined to agree with his aesthetic assessment—pasque flowers, particularly those selections that sport deep red or purple blossoms, are among spring's most dramatic harbingers. Because they're apt to get lost in the tumult of the border, it's best to plant them in a rock garden or some similar spot where their large bells, yellow stamens, and silky, finely divided foliage can be admired at close quarters. Dwarf daffodils and tulips would also look good in that kind of setting.

Tulipa 'Black Swan'
'Black Swan' single late tulip

PRONOUNCED **TEW-li-pa**

TYPE OF PLANT **Hardy bulb**

HEIGHT AND SPREAD **24–32 in. × 6–8 in.**

BLOOM TIME **Late spring**

ZONE **3–8**

Sun

Moderate

DARK-FLOWERED TULIPS have a lustrous sheen that makes them irresistible—the petals look as though they'd been fashioned from some rare and priceless silk. Seductive as they are, they need careful handling in the garden—a near-black flower will disappear against a dark background or against bare earth, and even when it's illuminated by bright sun, it needs contrasting partners to bring out its beauty. Russell Page, in his classic book *Education of a Gardener*, describes a planting in which masses of black and white tulips were underplanted with sky blue forget-me-nots (*Myosotis*). I can't think of a simpler or more thrilling combination. A more achievable scheme might pair 'Black Swan' with the bluish lilac tulip 'Bleu Aimable'. I suspect Page would approve.

Brown, Bronze, and Copper

**Japanese
cobra lily**

**Chocolate
cosmos**

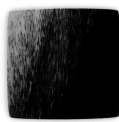

**'Zwanenburg Bronze'
snow crocus**

**Rusty
foxglove**

**Kamchatka
fritillary**

**Michael's
flower**

**'Chaffinch'
show auricula**

**'Autumn Colors'
black-eyed Susan**

**Giant
trillium**

**'Abu Hassan'
triumph tulip**

WE'RE IN CURIOUS TERRITORY HERE. In the garden, brown usually (but not always) means senescence or death; when it appears in a healthy, robust flower, it can cause a mild case of cognitive dissonance in the observer. It's worth suppressing that reaction, however, because brown and its allied shades can be marvelously warm and subtle, capable of infinite beguiling nuances. It helps if you think of brown as simply a dark version of orange; that also gives a clue about its best use in the garden: if something looks good with orange, it's more than likely to look good with brown.

Arisaema sikokianum

Japanese cobra lily

PRONOUNCED **air-uh-SEE-muh sih-koe-kee-AY-num**

TYPE OF PLANT **Hardy perennial**

HEIGHT AND SPREAD **12–20 in. × 16 in.**

BLOOM TIME **Mid-spring**

ZONE **4–8**

Light Shade

Full Shade

Moderate

NOT TOO LONG AGO THERE WAS A COBRA LILY craze in some segments of the gardening world. The most welcome result of this burst of enthusiasm was to make Japanese cobra lily more widely available and affordable. With its chocolate-colored spathe (the hooded part) and pure white spadix (the part that looks like a little marshmallow), it is, without doubt, the gem of the genus. Some individuals even have foliage that's striped with pink and silver. With such a distinctive plant, there's no point in getting fussy with companions. Plant as many of the cobra lily as you can afford, and then add some fresh green deciduous ferns (lady fern, *Athyrium filix-femina*; or maidenhair, *Adiantum pedatum*), and you'll be done.

Cosmos atrosanguineus
Chocolate cosmos

PRONOUNCED **KOS-mus at-ro-san-GWIN-ee-us**

TYPE OF PLANT **Tender perennial**

HEIGHT AND SPREAD **24–36 in. × 12–24 in.**

BLOOM TIME **Late spring to autumn**

ZONE **7–9**

NORTH AMERICAN NATIVE

Sun

Moderate

Light

CHOCOLATE COSMOS HAS A DOUBLE CLAIM to fame: first for its deep reddish-brown color and second for its fragrance, which is indeed reminiscent of chocolate. (The scent tends to be strongest in the early evening.) As tempting as it might be to view chocolate cosmos as a novelty, that would be doing it a disservice—given the velvety beauty of the flowers and the plant's ability to bloom for three months or longer, it deserves to rank with the cream of ornamentals. Although it can be grown in a container, it's much more vigorous and floriferous when grown in the ground. Striking foliage makes the best complement: 'Sparkling Burgundy' pineapple lily (*Eucomis*) for harmony, silver-and-bronze-leaved *Astelia* 'Westerland' for contrast.

Crocus chrysanthus 'Zwanenburg Bronze'

'Zwanenburg Bronze' snow crocus

PRONOUNCED **KROH-kus kry-ZAN-thus**

TYPE OF PLANT **Hardy bulb**

HEIGHT AND SPREAD **3–4 in. × 3–4 in.**

BLOOM TIME **Early spring**

ZONE **5–8**

Sun

Part Sun

Moderate

WELL BEFORE THE FAT DUTCH CROCUSES make their appearance, the snow crocuses poke up through the still-bare earth to cheer the winter-weary gardener. A quick glance at almost any bulb catalog will turn up white, purple, lilac, and pearly blue selections, but it's the yellows, especially those with brown markings on the reverse of the petals, that most effectively dispel the February gloom. There aren't too many suitable companions in bloom this early, but fortunately the netted irises (*Iris reticulata*) are, and their blue is the perfect counterpoint to 'Zwanenburg Bronze'. Another possibility is simply to plant other selections of snow crocus, in large groups of a single variety. Don't mix them up, or you'll get a visual mishmash.

Digitalis ferruginea

Rusty foxglove

PRONOUNCED **didge-ih-TAY-liss fair-oo-JIN-ee-uh**

TYPE OF PLANT **Hardy perennial**

HEIGHT AND SPREAD **36–72 in. × 12–18 in.**

BLOOM TIME **Mid- to late summer**

ZONE **4–10**

Sun

Part Sun

Moderate

MOST GARDENERS ARE WELL ACQUAINTED with purple foxglove (*Digitalis purpurea*), but there are many other members of the genus, some of them fascinating. Rusty foxglove richly deserves that description. Its narrow flower stalks can get as tall as six feet, and are crowded with small, yellowish bells, each of which is beautifully marked inside with copper pencilings. The plant's exclamation-point silhouette is as striking as the flower color, and should be exploited to the utmost when you're deciding how to use it. I'd like to see it combined with brown daylilies (*Hemerocallis*) and copper-colored New Zealand sedges (*Carex*)—the result would be living proof of the Power of Brown.

Fritillaria camschatcensis
Kamchatka fritillary

PRONOUNCED **frit-ih-LAIR-ee-uh kam-shat-SEN-sis**

TYPE OF PLANT **Hardy bulb**

HEIGHT AND SPREAD **8–16 in. × 12–18 in.**

BLOOM TIME **Mid- to late summer**

ZONE **3–8**

NORTH AMERICAN NATIVE

Light Shade

Heavy

THIS SOMBER PLANT'S COMMON NAME is a bit misleading, since it occurs abundantly in northwestern North America and Japan as well as in Russia. (If you like, you can also call it by the evocative name "black sarana.") The brown, bell-shaped flowers gain an extra dimension of mystery from the jet-black nectaries that cluster at the base of the stamens. Kamchatka fritillary blooms much later than most fritillaries, which extends the range of possible companion plants. I'd be leery of planting anything too flashy nearby; a few clumps of black mondo grass (*Ophiopogon planiscapus* 'Nigrescens') would be supremely simple and effective. Be careful never to let the soil dry out entirely; that spells certain death for the bulbs.

Fritillaria michailovskyi

Michael's flower

PRONOUNCED **frit-ih-LAIR-ee-uh mee-kile-OFF-skee-eye**

TYPE OF PLANT **Hardy bulb**

HEIGHT AND SPREAD **4–10 in. × 4–6 in.**

BLOOM TIME **Mid-spring**

ZONE **4–8**

Sun

Part Sun

Moderate

THIS FRITILLARY, ORIGINALLY FOUND in Turkey in 1904, disappeared from cultivation for more than fifty years before being rediscovered in 1965. Fortunately, micropropagation has now made it readily available and affordable. "Pert" isn't always a complimentary description, but it seems apt when applied to Michael's flower—the tubby, two-tone bells practically burst with cheer and jauntiness. If you want lots of them on each flower stem, try the selection 'Multiform'. (To my eye, it looks uncomfortably crowded.) Michael's flower has such a distinctive color scheme that it's best to repeat it in companion plants, with brown and yellow tulips and dwarf bearded irises. Bronze-colored violas would be nice, too.